Reviews

Having just read David's new book, I now understand why he was so successful, and I would highly recommend his work to anyone looking to improve business efficiency and effectiveness through improving relationships.
John Hanlon, Estates Director, HM Naval Base Clyde

David Fraser gets it! The struggle out there is the projection of the struggle in here. We can't begin to heal the world until we heal in here.
Stuart Hepburn, NLP Trainer

Excellent—an integrated system for effective relationships, drawing on several different domains and inspirations into a freshly unified approach. The structure is really good and clear and logical, and the content is equally useful in professional, social, and family contexts. Very readable. A dozen copies for family and close work colleagues, please.
Hillary Sillitto, Chartered Engineer

In addition to being a good "read through," this book is great to dip into when searching for some insight into what may be holding you back— there is a wealth of great content to help increase personal effectiveness.
Ian Laird, Managing Director, NiTech Solutions Ltd.

Hugely enjoyed reading this book! I love the stuff about relationships being more than communication skills. I enjoy and appreciate the honesty throughout. David draws attention to the qualities shown by good leaders, and I find that helpful and inspiring. I am moved by the spiritual depth of the writing.
The Rev. Scott S. McKenna

An excellent book, simply written. Very empowering.
Karen Mason, Leadership Coach

A very practical self-help book with the right amount of personal experience, academic background, and anecdotal evidence, and no slant toward either the male or female reader. Great for women in the workplace, especially where men predominate. The techniques are very helpful in levelling that particular playing field.
Morag Cook, Programme Manager (Public Sector)

Accessible and relevant. Each chapter has something that resonates with me ... and I suspect with anyone who wants practical ideas on how to work more effectively with others. Relationship Mastery: A Business Professional's Guide *is going on the Recommended Reading list for my courses!*
Florence Madden, Management Development Consultant

David Fraser reveals the essentials to successful relationships with colleagues, friends, and loved ones through his direct, easy-to-read style and use of very personal examples. Whether you are new to the subjects he writes about or are already a practitioner, you will learn something from this book.
Marnie Roadburg, NLP Practitioner, Retired Director of Disability Service, University of Edinburgh

Loved the honesty of the book and the anecdotes throughout. Especially impressed by the applications chapter.
Miriam King, Head of Group Operations (Public Sector)

Loved it! Very easy and interesting to read. Nice approach of being one of us and not claiming mastery of NLP. David keeps it simple.
Eleni Sarantinou, Life Coach

A stimulating read that has caused me to reflect and has influenced my approach to interactions both with my family and at work.
Julian Thomas, Senior Project Manager

The author has distilled the key elements of a number of disciplines, such as NLP, to produce a book that can be "used and abused" by the reader to succeed across a range of life's challenges—interact with it, learn from it, and apply it.
Brian Martin, Managing Director, Caltona Ltd.

A book rich in ideas. Easy to read and digest because of the excellent way it is structured. Having read the book, I will keep it on my bookshelf to be dipped into time and time again—I find with relationships, you have to keep working at them. Wish I'd had this book twenty years ago.
Tony Miller, Senior Lecturer, Robert Gordon University

Relationships matter in every walk of life, and a read through these pages will provide much to think about and many opportunities to change and improve. Good relationships are worth striving for.
Professor Sir Kenneth Calman
Chancellor, University of Glasgow

A work colleague said that it had "transformed" her approach. An inspiring book.
Gayle Cattanach, Owner, MAM Ltd.

David is deft at changing the language to easily understood layman psychology so you don't get hung up on jargon... Once I started reading, I must admit I couldn't put it down, mainly because it is simply fascinating stuff.
Lindsay Scott, Arras People

Easy to read and written in plain English with no psycho-babble. A book that everyone would benefit from reading.
Denise Knowles, Relationship Counsellor

An excellent book for anyone who wants better relationships with family, friends, and work colleagues. Intelligently written, well researched without being high-brow, and most of all practical. Easy to read but not simplistic. A book you will read and go back to many times.
Gillian Penrice, Doctor of Medicine

I learned a lot about myself, new ways of approaching conflict, and techniques for getting to the heart of the matter more easily. Loved the easy-to-read format, the personal examples, and the related quotes. Definitely a recommended read whether you're facing challenges in your personal or professional relationships.
Julie Wise, Wise 1 Coaching

A pleasure to have read David's book and even more importantly, to interact with him because he is authentic in his reflection of his book.
Marie Pijanowski, The Center for Social Connections

After a week, my two teenage boys seemed to mature and grow in the way they related to their younger siblings and their father and me.
Samantha Gluck, Owner, All Media Freelance LLC

Highly navigable, oozing common sense, and widely peppered with excellent—and not-so-obvious—guidance, plus being extremely practical and relevant to everyday situations. The whole experience of the book is absorbing and fun.
Michael Leathes, Director, International Mediation Institute

Very positive, helpful, and enlightening. Always pertinent and balanced, and even profound. Invaluable.
Harry Reid, author and former Editor, *The Herald*

Also by Dr David Fraser

The Mastery of Leadership: Presence and Practice in Transformational Change

Relationship Mastery

A Business Professional's Guide

Relationship Mastery

A Business Professional's Guide

Dr David Fraser

Tay Publishing

Relationship Mastery
A Business Professional's Guide
©2015 by Dr David Fraser

Published by Tay Publishing
Suite C, Milngavie Enterprise Centre, Ellangowan Court
Milngavie, Glasgow G62 8PH, Scotland, UK

First published by Visual Impressions Publishing in the USA 2011

Cover and text design by Janet Aiossa/www.adamhilldesign.us
Cover photograph by Elizabeth Handy/www.lizhandy.net

ISBN: 978-0-9932491-1-2

This book is intended to provide accurate and authoritative information on the subject matter covered. It is sold with the understanding that neither the publisher nor the author is engaged in rendering professional services with the publication of this book. If professional advice or other expert assistance is required, the services of a competent professional should be sought.

To our wonderful children,

and in memory of my parents

Kenneth and Hilary Fraser

Contents

Foreword

Relationships are important in all aspects of life, and this book sets out a range of ways for changing and improving them. In some ways, I feel very much part of this book. It contains many of my favourite quotations, and I even find I have a practice point related to me hidden away in the text. So many things struck a chord, from the sayings to the actions required. My favourite phrase from Robert Burns, "O wad some power the giftie gie us, to see oursels as ithers see us," is there, as is another, though in a slightly different form, "If your only tool is a hammer, then all your problems will be nails."

But relationships are not easy at times and require energy and work, together with the skills described in this book, to make them effective. As an engineer, David Fraser might have used the analogy provided by the concept of entropy, in which the state of a system falls into chaos without energy being supplied. In other words, things don't just happen, you have to make them happen and work at them. Relationships also require time for reflection and for thinking; hence my great sympathy for the method noted in the book of taking the dog for a walk. This act of moving and thinking with a silent friend with you to listen, but not respond, is very helpful. Beach walking with the waves and the movement of the tide is another way to find an opportunity to reflect and consider. We also need to recognise that we can be the cause of poor relationships, and a phrase I use about myself sometimes summarises this well: "I don't get stressed myself, but I think I am a carrier." We sometimes don't help!

One of the books that I have found helpful is *I and Thou* by Martin Buber, a Jewish theologian. He describes relationships in various ways. For example, there are "I and You" relationships, where knowledge of each other is recognised, but is no closer. In time, this may change to an "I and Thou" relationship, which really does become close, and, as he describes it, there is a "sharing of hearts" relevant to one of the later chapters in this book, on "Love." Relationships change, and a good example of this is of that between a master and student. In the beginning, it is "I and You," the master leading the student, but as the learning develops and the teacher recognises potential, so it changes to "I and Thou." As the learner surpasses the master, the great reward of the teacher becomes clear.

David Fraser's book provides a resource, a fund of methods, actions, and ideas. Relationships matter in every walk of life, and a read through these pages will provide much to think about and many opportunities to change and improve. Good relationships are worth striving for. They can provide a sense of belonging and improve personal value. I once wrote a long time ago about my experience of working and made the comment that you don't need to be nasty to get along in life or in business. It's possible to be nice and still make things happen and change the world. I still think that is true today.

Professor Sir Kenneth Calman
Chancellor
University of Glasgow

There is nothing more powerful than an idea whose time has come.

–Victor Hugo

Prologue: An invitation

In the time it has taken me to bring this book to fruition, I have frequently questioned my preparedness to write about getting along well with other people. There's always another book to read, another course to attend, another speaker to hear; or another upset at home, another disagreement at work, and yes, even another quarrel that seems to say that I am no more qualified to put forward skills for relating to other people than the next person. And yet I have seen the benefits that friends and colleagues have gained from this material; I know the difference the ideas have made to my life and what I have achieved using them; and I realise the things that don't go well just confirm the importance of interpersonal skills.

Getting along with people reliably and effectively and achieving the results we want is difficult and takes more effort than we commonly admit. Social interaction is complex and apparently unpredictable. Up until the age of about 40, I didn't really understand what was going on in my relationships with other people. My career at that time was limited not by intellect, knowledge, or leadership skills, but by shortcomings in the way I dealt with other people. It wasn't that my people skills were dreadful, just that certain mistakes I was making were undermining the rest of what I was doing and holding me back as a result. At about the same time, I was making a mess of my second marriage.

I struggled with these twin problems for some years without any great progress. By what now seems like great good fortune, and a slender thread to the beginning of this story, I was introduced to Neuro-Linguistic Programming (NLP)—a powerful collection of knowledge stuck with an off-putting label, in my eyes anyway. Whether this learning saved my marriage, I can't say, because I don't know if we would have come apart without it, but it definitely earned its place at the centre of our family system.

At first, my focus was a personal one, though I soon understood that the new skills were a great answer to the question of how to get along with other people in all situations, including at work. Other aspects of psychology are, of course, important to relationships too. I have included some of them here. But NLP has a systematic character and emphasises things we can actually do. It forms the backbone of the practical approach I have since gathered for getting along with the people we need to get along with.

For a long time, I saw relationship skills as merely supportive of our other professional and personal expertise—something complementary and deserving a proportion of our attention, but only a proportion. I realised recently that I was understating the case. An ability to relate well to other people brings so many benefits, and the necessary skills are sufficiently easy to learn, that putting their development first makes complete sense. It's even tempting to suggest that you can forget everything else. Far from being a troublesome area, developing our ability to get along with the people we need to get along with can be an easy way to succeed, if we have the right tools. This is true whether we are thinking of professional or personal life.

In starting this book, I wondered whether to focus on the workplace or on the home. In reality, the question is moot because it's all the same in the end. At the fundamental level we're interested in here, the skills are the same. Something learned in one context applies to the other. Anyway, we only have so much time to invest, so we're better off learning skills we can use everywhere.

In my experience, marriage and family life presents some of the biggest challenges we face in our lives. We're not supposed to talk about the problems much, and we tend to pretend everything's fine, and perhaps it is. Or maybe we could benefit from more skills.

My wife and I have three children, one of whom has autism. In early 2009, when our son was four, we visited several special needs schools in our area to decide which would be the most suitable for him. Our son has relatively mild autism and the potential to overcome many, if not all, of his difficulties. In contrast, we met some children with various conditions who are severely challenged. Our visit was at the time of a war in the Middle East, when many innocent children and adults were killed or maimed and made dependent for what seemed very tenuous reasons. The contrast between the efforts to make the most of the lives of the naturally disadvantaged children at the special school and the man-made suffering elsewhere was striking and a reminder, if one was needed, that we haven't yet established a way to get along on this planet of ours.

I was deeply affected by our visit to the special needs school. I wonder still what goes on in the heads of the little children we met, some of them held upright in special wheelchairs because they couldn't hold their heads up for themselves. I can picture one boy's face in particular, looking at me—I believe, looking for love. Now I might even say looking into my soul. The experience taught me a lesson I will never forget: If I have the ability and inclination to do something in my life, I should—must, even—because not everyone has the same chance. That "something" is to share what I have learned about getting along with people.

One of the challenges children with autism face is learning social skills, because of their difficulties with language and lack of awareness of other people's thoughts and feelings. As their parents, we are faced with the task of teaching them interpersonal skills starting from the very beginning. Unlike their "typical" peers, children with autism don't learn spoken language or social interaction for themselves. For the parents, that experience heightens awareness of how typical adults go on learning to interact with other people throughout their lives—or the consequences if they don't.

My focus here is on individuals and their relationships, but in fact, the messages apply equally at the corporate, national, or global scale. Whether the learning can spread that far, I have little idea, but if somehow the world adopted these skills, we would have many fewer problems. As a friend said: "Wouldn't the wheels turn?" Wouldn't they just.

In 2009, I participated in a meeting to discuss the threat we all face in the form of potentially catastrophic global warming. The meeting was led by Alastair McIntosh, author of *Hell and High Water.* At one point, Alastair said: "The thing is we need better relationships in the world." An insistent, "I must get my book finished," went around in my head for the rest of the evening.

The tone of the meeting itself was realistic, but I thought excessively so. In coaching, there is a belief that if we limit our aspiration for our client, we will limit their achievement. They may achieve beyond our limiting belief, but it will be in spite of us, not because of us. I suggested that the group was collectively in the role of "coach" and the world was the "client." So, limiting our belief about what is possible for the world in relation to global warming limits our ability to make a difference. Applying that thinking to my own work, I choose to believe that there are no limits to what can be achieved with this book.

So, for all that my learning about relationships and connecting with other people is a continuing journey and I write as much as translator and collector rather than originator, the current report on my travels is offered here. What I have experienced so far has been a great help to me. I believe there is much here to help you too.

In fact, I'm inviting you to come on the journey.

The need for relationship mastery

Getting along with people, unblocking your life

Before *You may:*	After *You will:*
✘ Be seen as "difficult"	✔ Understand what's going on in all your relationships
✘ Find relationships a bit of a mystery	✔ Connect with other people quickly, reliably, and easily
✘ Be unaware of how you come across	✔ Have successful relationships at work, home, and elsewhere
✘ Make frequent mistakes with other people	✔ Be confident with others
✘ Struggle to connect with people you meet	✔ Do business with the people you want to do business with
✘ Have problems in your relationship with your partner or your family	✔ Mend relationships that aren't working
✘ Feel you're not fulfilling your potential	✔ Release the brakes on career and personal progress
✘ Be unsure of what you want	✔ Be seen as interesting, friendly, and fun to be with
✘ Act out of fear	✔ Get along with people with a lot less effort
✘ Lose business	✔ Leverage up everything else in your life
✘ Waste your talents	✔ Be a success
✘ Miss out on promotion and be overtaken in your career	✔ Act out of love
✘ Have low self-esteem	✔ Be peaceful
✘ Think you're a failure	

The need for relationship mastery

Mastery, in the context of this book, means the attainment of thorough knowledge or skill, and hints at a power that is controlled and used with wisdom and integrity, and a discipline that can be relied upon in good times and bad. Mastery alludes to openness to continued learning and a lifelong journey. What more appropriate word then to use for that most important of subjects—our ability to relate successfully to other people?

Most of us could have much more success and happiness at work and in our personal lives if we developed our relationship mastery and paid a bit more attention to the skills we use in our dealings with other people and the state of mind we bring to the process.

Those in the know have systematic ways to get along with other people. If you're not aware of what they're doing, their results can look like magic. Don't be fooled—the methods they use are surprisingly quick, reliable, easy to learn, and latent in all of us.

For some people, learning these skills can feel like an impossible task, while others believe it to be a completed process. It's neither, and yet these skills are one of the few things we can rely on in an ever-changing world. They can also save us a lot of time.

Not only are these skills easy to learn, they can be used in any situation. You don't need to think "this is such-and-such a situation, so I have to use such-and-such a script." You can have a system that is relevant whatever the circumstances—whether it involves your career or personal life, it makes little difference. Success at home and success at work go hand-in-hand. As Parker J. Palmer says in *The Courage to Teach*: "The personal can never be divorced from the professional."

The classic book on interpersonal relationships is Dale Carnegie's *How to Win Friends and Influence People*, which has been very widely read since its publication in 1937. Dale Carnegie refers to a study that found, after health, adults' second interest is "how to understand and get along with people." He had been "searching for years to discover a practical, working handbook on human relations" and since no such book existed, he wrote one, hoping that it would be liked. By 2006, more than 16 million people had liked it enough to buy it.

So why do we need another book? Well, more knowledge is at our disposal now, 70 or so years later, and there's much more to offer in the way of suggestions for "use immediately in business, in social contacts, and in the home," as the need was expressed all those years ago. Meanwhile, if you take a look around, it would seem that Dale Carnegie's book hasn't solved every problem in interpersonal relations, great job though he did, and perhaps the need is even greater now than it was then.

So what more can we do? Well, we have the understanding now to go a little deeper into what happens between people and gain enough insight to make proper sense of what is going on. Only then can we learn, understand, and act at just the right level of abstraction to be confident we are working in the full knowledge of what's happening. Until we *do* look a bit closer, individually and collectively, and develop a deeper awareness and skill, our relationships aren't going to get much better. We're in the territory of Daniel Goleman's *Emotional Intelligence* here, but we need something to tell us what to actually do. We need the "how."

All sorts of people I speak to have found that dealing with others doesn't go as smoothly as they would like. They would welcome some insight. Perhaps that's your story too. I believe that not only does our ability to relate to other people determine much of what happens in our lives, it's also one of the things we can most easily do something about, if we adopt an effective approach. Working on our relationship skills is an effective way to professional and personal success, and a vital part of our personal mastery—the name Peter Senge applied to our commitment to lifelong learning and, as he put it, the "discipline of continually clarifying and deepening our personal vision."

Before we start on the details, however, we'd better address the question of how I, a Scottish engineer, got involved in all this. Haven't I lost my way somewhere? Well, yes, I probably did go wrong, but in a different sense....

A starting point

The need to do a better job of getting along with people took a serious turn for me ten years ago after a conversation with my then boss. "David," he said, "certain things you're doing are holding you back, but I can't tell you what they are."

"Thanks very much, Bob. That's really helpful," I replied, as if it's completely normal to be told you aren't getting along with people as well as you need to, but not what to do about it. About that time, I was also described as both "difficult" and "not demanding enough." I've been working on a systematic way of relating to other people ever since.

I'm pleased to report that feedback now is more positive. For example, a client recently told me: "One of the reasons things have worked so well is that you listen, understand the problem, and help us do our work. You get people to talk to each other who wouldn't do that naturally." That was on a large and complex project. Another added: "You're never confrontational at all and are able to point people in the right direction without getting their backs up."

A friend said: "You have moved from being a 'tell' person, to being an 'ask and listen' person. In particular, I notice that you are much more aware of the ebb and flow of attention between yourself and others, and aim to achieve an overall balance. I don't think you paid attention to this when I first knew you."

This book is about what has made the difference. With it, you can learn in a few months what has taken me ten years. Without it? Well, I wouldn't want to go back there.

Before we go any further, I want to state that I am still perfectly capable of making a mess of things, especially at home. Let's be clear though: The problems start when I don't apply what I've learned, not when I do.

Reasons to get along with people

We need other people to be truly ourselves. Carl Jung

You might not be sure that getting along with people matters, but if we're careless in the way we deal with other people, we so easily damage our prospects of success by causing irritation or resentment in those whose help we need to achieve our results—make the sale, decide on the course of action, buy the service, complete the project, have the holiday we want, or whatever.

From the way many behave, it seems they've decided that getting along with people is less important than looking out for themselves, but paying attention to their dealings with other people is the very thing they need to do to make the most of their circumstances. If we go about disregarding the human dimension, we build up resistance against ourselves that makes it harder to achieve what we want to achieve. We can perhaps fight our way to what we want—and some seem to prefer that approach—but it's such hard work that our success will be limited by the energy required. It's much easier to have people working with you rather than against you. From time to time, our objectives may be in tension or even conflict with what somebody else wants, but we'll achieve a better outcome if we invest in the relationship despite the difficulty. Here are two examples:

Formal authority isn't enough

If you manage people in your work, you might think: "I can just tell them what I want, so why do I need to change my approach? Why do I need to worry about relationships when I have authority?"

Only a small proportion of the people you deal with report to you. Suppose you have the traditional span of control of about seven. You probably interact with at least 100 people altogether, so at most 10 percent of the people you need to relate to actually work for you. Authority is no help with bosses, peers, partners, customers, and most other interested parties.

Even with your own staff, you are likely to get better results using effective relationship skills. Relying only on your authority is expensive in goodwill and energy, and employees are less willing than in the past to subject themselves unconditionally to being managed. It's much better to build personal power through relationship skills than rely on a finite positional authority you may not always have.

Progress happens when interests are balanced

Eventually, we need to organise around an outcome where interests are in balance. Progress happens in the middle ground. As individuals, we are vulnerable to a trap. If we're at one of the extremes of an issue, we risk being left out of the solution. If we're not careful, we become conditioned that tension and conflict are the norm and productive relationships secondary.

We need to avoid being led by the media and their love of an argument, the more polarising the better. If we're in the mood, we might be entertained, but we must take care not to adopt their behaviour in our lives. (Of course, behind the scenes, media organisations themselves are dependent on people interacting effectively to deliver their output.)

We live in a complex world

Few of us work in traditional, hierarchical organisations. Most operate in complex environments with multiple internal and external relationships through which we achieve our results. Very few work settings have a clear unity of purpose that aligns all the contributors without tension. Much more usual is a coalition of interests to deliver a higher objective. For example, a complex alliance of budget holders, managers, administrators, consultants, hospital doctors, primary care professionals, nurses, auxiliaries, receptionists, porters, other paramedical specialists, and a variety of service providers all collaborate to deliver healthcare to the nation. Success for the individuals and the organisations depends on the relationship skills of all the participants, very few of whom have direct authority over one another.

Ways to get along with other people are poorly understood. Companies use phrases such as "relationship marketing," "customer relationship management," and "key account selling" with little idea what that means person-to-person and have few methods to help employees develop the implied people skills.

In our personal lives, we organise our affairs, raise our families, look after relatives, and pursue our leisure interests through a circle of people whose help we need to achieve what we want within the limited time and money we have available. Achieving anything significant in a family setting involves balancing opposed interests and finding common ground, just like at work.

Family life is tough going if we don't get along

Relationship problems at home have the potential to dominate our lives. It's hard to be successful at work if things are going badly elsewhere. Conventionally, we're expected to keep our personal lives and our working lives apart, but really that is a nonsensical idea. Problems in our family lives have such a deep effect that we can hardly help but be distracted. Stable relationships at home with effective ways to resolve issues can help us greatly in being productive at work.

We can leverage our existing skills

One major benefit of improving our relationship skills is that it helps just about everything else we do because so much involves interacting with other people. The reward is higher than most other options for developing ourselves. Improving people skills is often said to be difficult, but with the right tools, it's easy and inexpensive.

Get along with people anywhere, anytime

As we shall see, we can adopt an approach to relationship mastery that applies unchanged in a whole range of situations from the plainest of domestic settings through to the most complex of organisations (or, if you prefer, from the most complex of domestic settings through to the plainest of organisational ones), including these situations:

- Working effectively with colleagues
- Building relationships with customers and suppliers
- Maintaining the support of stakeholders
- Being effective in all kinds of meetings
- Dealing with the elaborate relationships involved in large organisations
- Managing complex organisations such as public-private partnerships
- Collaborating on a shared purpose
- Improving relationships with partners and other family members
- Parenting
- Enjoying leisure interests
- Obtaining the service we want in shops and restaurants
- Being a supportive friend

We can have a system that is a foundation for all of these contexts and more.

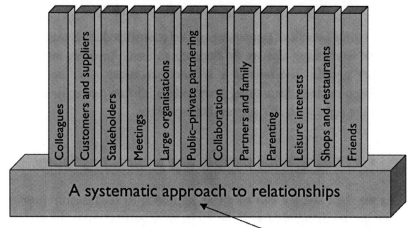

A systematic approach to relationships

Working here has the biggest pay-off
An inside track – "All you really need"

You might think it a stretch to ask one system to cover so much, but what's the use of a universal approach that isn't universal? The whole point is to have a method that's always relevant and to invest our energies in learning skills that will benefit us in all situations, rather than in just one or two aspects of our lives.

Honing your relationship skills can give you the confidence that you have particular insights or value to add in just about any situation involving people at any level—whether you're a distinguished leader, an ordinary man or woman in the street, or someone conducting affairs of state. In fact, these skills can be applied everywhere you deal with people who have different views and with whom forming effective relationships is by no means straightforward.

More of the same won't help

The significant problems we have cannot be solved at the same level of thinking with which we created them. Albert Einstein

More of what worked yesterday isn't always the answer. In fact, it may make the situation worse. What got us to where we are today may be the very thing that will trap us or undermine us now. As Richard Bandler put it: "The processes which allow us to accomplish the most extraordinary and unique human activities are the same processes which block our further growth."

We can access many excellent sources on communication skills, but most are focused on our end of the equation: being assertive, getting what we want, putting our point across, having impact, persuading people, winning the argument, and so on. When it's the relationship that matters, none of these one-sided approaches is the answer. More assertiveness, persuasion, logic, impact, and influence aren't going to solve the problem—that's not the right kind of mastery. We're looking in the wrong place. Putting it bluntly, we need to back off.

Many books promise to help you get other people to do what you want them to do, but that sounds to me like manipulation. If you value the relationship, you have a problem of integrity: How can you simultaneously respect the relationship and bend the other person to what you want, unless it's what they want as well? To put the relationship first, you have to start with a different attitude. You need to think of getting other people to do what *they* want in such a way that you meet your needs as well—a subtle but important difference.

A word on sales

If your job involves selling, you may think sales is all about getting other people to do what you want. I'd rather look at it this way: Selling involves convincing other people to buy the products or services they need or want. Personally, I've never been able to sell people things that I don't believe are right for them (and I probably can't help you do that either).

Persuading other people to do what we want may bring us material results in the short term, but not lasting relationships. That's the big change you can make: a shift from pushing and pulling for what you want to a balance with other people that results in a flow in your relationships and greater success in the long run. Furthering your own aims isn't the way to get along with other people.

As Ted Nicholas says in *Magic Words that Grow Your Business*: "Ninety-seven percent of conventional wisdom is wrong." The majority of people achieve average results and if you do what they do, your outcome will be the same. If you want something better, you'll need to do something different. The question is, "What?" The answer is the subject of this book and also the opportunity for you.

The people who succeed are those who have formed the habit of doing the things others don't like to do. Albert E.N. Gray

We could also remember the definition of insanity as doing the same things and expecting different results, or as somebody said once: "Only dead fish go with the flow." When you're in the three percent bucking conventional wisdom, expect to feel out of step.

The key is turning our focus outward to our relationships with others. This we need to do to be a success. Ironically, the predominance of books on personal development compared to books on how to relate to other people demonstrates the need for this shift. The typical personal development text has only a chapter or two on relationships. We're so inward-looking that most of our books are about ourselves. Of course we need to work on *how we are*, but that's for when we are alone, not when we are relating to other people.

Don't take it from me, decide for yourself

You don't need to take my word for any of this. You can take time to convince yourself. You will likely be sceptical at first, as I was. Some aspects require us to question the old certainties and reverse our habits, which can seem unsettling and unnatural. The skills we cover work and work very well. In fact, they work so well, it's difficult to explain why they're not more commonly used. Or perhaps more people are using them than we realise and we're in danger of being left behind.

Some of what works appears counter-intuitive, and putting it into practice may involve eliminating many of our habitual behaviours. Here's a preview in the form of the first of many "Steps to take:"

Steps to take

 To have influence, don't try to influence people directly. The more you try, the less they will pay attention, whereas the more you focus on others and their needs, the more they will be open to you. As Dale Carnegie wrote: "The only way on earth to influence other people is to talk about what they want and show them how to get it."

Communication skills are not enough

Communication skills as commonly understood are only a part of relationship skills. Their context is a fleeting interaction in which we seek an outcome there and then. If we see communication as the whole story, we miss an opportunity.

The word "relationship" implies an ongoing connection with other people; what is there between us and what remains when we part; what we mean when we say we "know" someone. Building a relationship happens through time and may involve sacrificing what we want now for something greater in the future.

Relationships are more than the interactions that take place. They continue when there is no contact, even when all possibility of interaction has passed. Communication skills emphasise the speaker and the message rather than the quality of the ongoing connection. An ability to put our point across may be the very thing that gets us into trouble if we out-communicate those we are dealing with. The more articulate we are, the more we need to strengthen our relationship skills to match.

However, mere communication is difficult and often ineffective and insufficient for what it is intended to achieve, especially in awkward circumstances. We'll look later at some of the reasons why. Working on the underlying relationships is a good way to ease its path.

There's more going on between us than we realise

What you don't realise is that most of your life is unconsciously determined.
Milton Erickson

One of the reasons communication can be difficult is because much of what happens is outside our conscious awareness. Among other things, our emotions affect what we do and say, and we're not that aware of their effect on us.

We can think of two dimensions to relationships: the rational and conscious, and the emotional and unconscious. If there are emotional drivers in a relationship—and there usually are—no amount of movement in the rational and conscious direction is going to take us from the origin "o" where we start to a solution at point "x," say, that needs movement in the emotional and unconscious dimension as well.

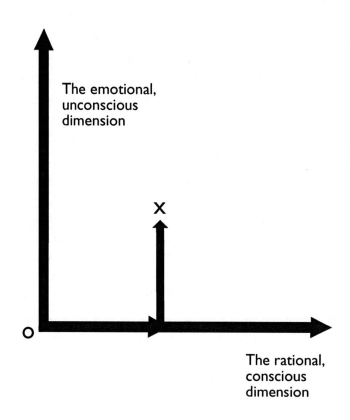

Lots of communication takes place without us really noticing. Often, our conscious minds talk about something relatively unimportant while our unconscious minds converse on something more important, such as how we feel about each other. Our world is rather dominated by left-brain thinking where words, measurement, and logic are pre-eminent, while creative, sensing, and feeling right-brain aspects are suppressed. Therein lies the opportunity.

Steps to take

 Let's convince you right now that more is going on than you realise: Try spelling a word that you find difficult. As you say each letter, notice whether your eyes move (even momentarily) and, if so, in which direction. It's likely your eyes move up briefly either to your right or your left—most likely left if you are right-handed. Try looking up to the opposite side and spelling another difficult word. Chances are you'll find one side helps you remember and the other side is physically uncomfortable—a kind of eye strain.

Most of us spell difficult words by visualising them, and to access the remembered image, our eyes move up and to our left. We move our eyes up and to the right when we are creating images.

You may have come across this before. Some, mostly left-handed people, have their "eye-accessing" the other way around.

Here's another one: Stand on one leg, with that knee slightly bent to help you balance. Move your other foot above the ground in a clockwise direction and keep it circling. Once you have established that pattern, try drawing the figure 6 in front of you using the hand on the same side of your body as the circling foot and notice what happens. Try it now.

Most people find that their foot starts circling the same way as the six is drawn—counter-clockwise. When we attempt the exercise, our unconscious mind intervenes. If we use the hand on the opposite side from the foot, the job is easier, with less interference between the two tasks.

Our unconscious mind controls much more than we think, yet we pay little attention to it. What else is going on that you're not aware of?

We can learn to work with the emotional and unconscious dimensions and come to treat them as a route to solving problems rather than something to be suppressed. Working with our own and others' emotions can be a source of advantage rather than something to be avoided. After all, everyone has feelings. They may not show, but they're there. Men are perhaps particularly inclined to put too much faith in the power of reason and logic.

Accepting that we need to engage with the emotional and the subjective can be a stretch for many of us. We have been trained to value objective criteria and approaches and disconnect ourselves emotionally from the thing we want to study. In order to learn about ourselves and our relationships, however, we have no choice but to engage with the subjective. The physical sciences are often presented as objective, and yet as Richard Bandler points out, the sciences change over time even though the world stays the same, so it must be that there is a subjective element, even to the physical sciences.

Wake up before it's too late

For all the refinement of our education, we receive little or no instruction in how to be effective with other people. Our parents and teachers bring us up to be polite and fit in with the world, but that's about as far as it goes. Various schools would no doubt protest that they turn out individuals with "character," but that is not necessarily helpful in relationships and may be part of the problem.

Like many children with a similar background, I was encouraged to have an enhanced sense of identity and a belief in my own success. As a basis for achievement, this method of education is a powerful model. On the other hand, our relationships may suffer as a consequence of our sense of superiority and the priority given to achievement. That was very much my experience. We need to improve our people skills to compensate and learn some humility.

Institutions of further and higher education usually make little or no attempt to develop our ability to interact with other people. Once young adults emerge from school, their people skills are considered a matter for them alone. When we engage in the world of work, the consequences of poor relationship skills can be sudden and severe, although we may be lucky and encounter someone who helps us learn. If we had an extensive education and training that emphasised analytical, logical, and rational thinking in vocational subjects, we may have an even bigger challenge. In 1937, Lowell Thomas wrote of Dale Carnegie's audience: "They had poured over books, believing that knowledge alone was the open sesame to financial and professional rewards. But a few years in the rough-and-tumble of business and professional life had brought sharp disillusionment." Not much has changed in three-quarters of a century.

We may be taught leadership, management, communication, and so forth, but very rarely the fundamental interpersonal skills that underpin everything and have the most effect. Of course, the matter is delicate, and we reject clumsy attempts to guide us that seem to strike at the core of who we are, but the tragedy—and it is a tragedy—is that we can go through years of our lives with the people around us all well aware of our mistakes, but nobody ever tells us or helps us notice. In my case, it took until the age of 41 to find a reliable solution to this problem of getting along with people, and I could easily have missed it.

Many people, perhaps the majority, live out their lives without ever learning a few simple things about themselves that would have made a vast difference. And you know what? Everybody around them talks about their faults, but they remain unaware: "David can be difficult," "Karen's a bit snippy," or "John's so negative," and in fact, play along with their patterns and in so doing reinforce them. If we knew how others experienced us, surely we would want to make changes. We can escape from all this by taking responsibility ourselves for how we come across. There is a way.

You might say this all is just about growing up. If so, we need a way to accelerate the process.

Release the brakes, unblock your life

A good way to start improving our lives is to stop messing them up. Richard Koch

Most of us are held back to some extent by mistakes with other people. I definitely was—in fact still am, but less so—and it was frustrating until I understood why. We're reluctant to admit that we could learn something— anything—to make us more effective with other people, even though that can be our biggest challenge. Our skills are apparently complete. Maybe we just don't realise we're making mistakes. I used to think my interpersonal approach was effective and not holding me back in any way until I learned, at times painfully, that this assumption was wrong.

We tend to assume we are good at relationships, even though we see people around us making mistakes of which they are not aware. Perhaps we're not as versatile and skilled in relationships as we think we are. A typical example is someone regarded as "difficult" and whose mind seems to be closed to learning anything or to admitting that he might have a problem. Another is the person in authority who fears that being open to change will undermine her power when, of course, the reverse is the case. Ironic, when these people could perhaps benefit the most, as could the organisations they lead.

From the example file

📁 As a manager, Peter thinks he is expected to assert what he wants all the time and be dismissive of others' needs. He talks at people. Colleagues avoid him and turnover of his staff is high. He is excluded from interacting with customers at senior level because he lacks the necessary tact. He experiences his world of work as a battlefield.

📁 Angela is forceful with her opinions at work and is difficult to help. She is very knowledgeable, but her career is stuck because she has made too many enemies. She says she gets on well with people.

📁 Joe always seems to be making difficulties, and any problem is always someone else's fault. The consequences are a trial for everyone. He seems unaware of his reputation.

📁 Having said his piece in meetings, Alex turns his attention to the latest email or text message. His fellow directors wonder how to engage with him.

📁 "Tim's people skills are poor," his colleagues whisper, but it seems no one has ever told him.

(These are real examples, as are all the others to come, although the names have been changed.)

What mistakes might *you* be making? How would you know?

We can safely admit a lack of knowledge about a subject or skill for a practical task, but conceding that we could be better at relationships seems to be harder, as if we are expected just to know how to be skilful with other people. Perhaps the sheer difficulty makes us reticent, but as Frank Farrelly and Jeff Brandsma put it: "Life is like piano lessons. In the acquisition of any skill, including social skills, one starts off ignorant and makes obvious mistakes. In this process, there is no possible way *not* to make mistakes, and since this is so, one either needs a teacher to point out mistakes or learns to monitor his own behaviour without being devastated emotionally."

We find it easier to admit a problem once we are aware of a solution, when the issue can be acknowledged in safety and tackled. People often say something like, "I could use some of that with so and so," but they only allude to the challenge when the solution is in sight. Curiously, providing a way to work on relationship skills makes it acceptable to admit to weaknesses, to work on them, and to talk about the subject. I suggest you make a virtue of working on your ability to relate to other people. Respect comes to those who have the courage.

Our first reaction on realising that we know less than we thought about getting along with people is usually one of embarrassment and fear, but we may just have discovered the key to a better future. Because interpersonal skills leverage almost everything else we do, the bigger the gap we find between where we are now and where we could be, the more we have to gain.

On the one hand, the more resistant you are to reviewing your approach, the bigger the opportunity is likely to be. On the other hand, if you are skilful with people, the chances are you could be much, much better. And it's a comparatively easy way to get ahead. Are you going to overcome the habits that hold you back, or will you let the rest of your life be constrained by them?

You can change now; there's no need to wait

We can stop trying to change other people. It's a waste of time and energy, and our attempts are annoying. We're likely to just end up in a power struggle. We can only change ourselves, not others, so to change our relationships, the only option is to do or be something different ourselves. Fortunately, we don't need anyone else to do this. The changes we can make on our own have dramatic, highly beneficial, and rapid effects on our relationships with others and on how they behave toward us.

To have good relationships with other people, we need a good relationship with ourselves—to be peaceful inside. Most of us, however, are interdependent beings and can't delay interacting with the world around us until we are perfect within. In fact, working on our relationships can often help us within ourselves. Change on the outside may unblock us on the inside. We often need the other half of the picture, the half experienced by other people, to see how to sort ourselves out.

Only in relationship with other people can we be fulfilled and enabled to grow.
Sydney Rosen

Success with other people and personal growth go hand-in-hand in a balanced, iterative process. Working on our relationships without addressing our own issues is a recipe for frustration. Like much else, the key is balance.

We may be shocked to find that improving our relationships means we need to change. We say things like, "I got to where I am today by being who I am," or "That's just the way I am." These things are all choices—possibly choices we made a long time ago and perhaps unconsciously, but still choices, so we can revisit them if we want. Our current approach may serve us well, but it limits us too. Remaining who we are may stop us from moving on. Growth lies on the far side of feedback and learning. Situations with other people can and should cause us to reflect. Much of what we achieve is with, through, or for other people, and the sum state of our relationships determines our level of success.

Steps to take

 List ten people you interact with. Rate each relationship one to three for quality (low, medium, or high) and multiply this by another score (one to three) for importance to get a weighted score. Now add up all ten weighted scores. Dividing the result by 10 (the number of people on the list) and by 9 (the maximum possible score for each) gives a single measure for your relationship "stock" as a percentage of the maximum possible score in which all your relationships would be both important and of high quality. Here is an example:

Relationship with	Quality	Importance	Weighted score
John Ward	3	3	9
Margaret Murray	2	3	6
Karen Smith	3	2	6
James Hall	1	3	3
Stephen Watson	1	2	2
Lynn Hood	2	3	6
Alison Todd	1	1	1
Mike Jones	3	2	6
Tim Houston	3	1	3
Fiona Wilson	2	3	6
Total score			48
As a percentage			48 ÷ (10x9) = 53%

You may realise some relationships need attention and changes in the score over time might cause you to reflect on the reasons and take action as a result.

Relationship Mastery

Repeating the exercise for all your current, active contacts would give a fuller picture. That's probably 100 to 150 people.

As well as being a measure of the value of your contacts to you, the score would also be a measure of your value to your network.

The number of people we can meaningfully stay in touch with is limited to about 150, according to Malcolm Gladwell, and once you reach the limit, you can only enhance your network in two ways: by replacing contacts with more important or more diverse ones (which we do from time to time) and by improving the quality of the connections you choose to maintain. An effective approach to relationships will obviously help.

When we run into trouble and need support, as we surely will from time to time, the stronger our network—that is, the more friends we have—the more easily we will overcome our difficulties.

Soft skills?

The phrase "soft skills" is sometimes used in the context of relationships, meaning nebulous or indefinable, lacking in "edge," perhaps even of secondary importance and not to be taken too seriously. This need not—and should not—be the case.

Building and maintaining relationships is a critical life skill, and sometimes the process can be challenging. Situations may arise where a degree of robustness is required and the person on the receiving end may feel they have had anything but a "soft" experience. Relationship skills are not about being weak with people or being liked necessarily. We may need to be demanding from time to time.

The label "soft skills" seems also to imply the impossibility of a structured or systematic approach. On the contrary, as we shall see, relationships can be approached methodically. Use of the word "soft" can be misleading and is better avoided. Something that matters so much deserves to be discussed seriously and precisely.

Gather confidence and self-esteem

When we develop our skills with other people, our relationships improve and we also gain confidence. Our self-esteem increases, making us more appealing to others. When we continue to refine our approach successfully, our results again improve, reinforcing a helpful cycle.

We improve our skills for dealing with other people. We do more of what works and less of the rest

Our confidence and our relationships with other people improve

Our self-esteem improves as we have more success in our relationships

As our self esteem improves we become more attractive to other people

Confidence depends on all sorts of things, but it's a great help if we feel well equipped to relate to people and have a system on which we can rely. With the right tools, getting along with people does not have to be difficult. Blocks in our relationships, and so in our lives, can be overcome. It's an easy way to success, and having realised the benefit, we're well on our way. We just need a reliable, systematic approach.

The need for relationship mastery

In summary

- Getting along with people is vital to success.

- Shortcomings in our relationship skills blight our lives.

- Communication skills are not enough.

- Persuasion, assertiveness, and logic aren't in themselves the answer.

- We need to do something different.

- The key is to shift our focus outward, away from ourselves, and onto our relationships with other people.

- We can be systematic in our approach.

- By improving our relationship skills, we can unblock our lives and be a success.

Relating to you

- What would change if you enhanced your relationship skills?

- What's the biggest learning you have taken from this chapter?

A
systematic
approach

Using the available intelligence

Before	After
Before *You may:*	**After** *You will:*
✗ Be sceptical about practical psychology	✔ Have a sense of the respected origins of the material in this book
✗ Wonder if the material in this book has a grounding in established principles	✔ Understand that NLP is really about the study of ourselves
✗ Be frustrated with "quick fix" approaches that don't deliver transformational change	✔ Apply a realistic timescale to acquiring the skills
	✔ Understand that you need to practise and take action
	✔ Appreciate the merit of a systematic approach
	✔ Find your own evidence of success
	✔ Act with integrity

A systematic approach

Everything should be made as simple as possible, but not simpler.
Albert Einstein

Put a problem in front of engineers, and they will look for a solution. It's what we do. We also like to work at the level of the underlying principles so that we can learn something once and use it many times. That's the requirement here. We want a practical system we can apply to our relationships with other people that will give us more success with more people more of the time. We want the system to be concise enough to remember and universal enough to be reliable. We want to understand what's going on under the surface so that we can act at a deeper level in the most effective and economical way, using a set of skills that's independent of the context. That's pretty much what NLP does, despite its unpromising name.

What is Neuro-Linguistic Programming (NLP)?

We form habits or patterns through repetition of what we think, say, and do. Some of those habits work well for us and some of them don't. Typically, some that used to work for us don't any more or we may wish to learn something new. In either case, by understanding and changing the patterned behaviour, we can improve our outcomes. NLP is a powerful way to do that. At the simplest level, that is essentially it.

When I first learned NLP, I thought, "Here's a great answer to the problem of getting along with other people." Five years had gone by since the conversation with Bob I mentioned earlier, and to be frank, I had taken some wrong turns in my life.

I don't know why so few have written about succeeding in relationships by systematically applying a bit of simple, practical psychology. Perhaps I see a relevance that others haven't noticed or seen fit to point out. It is said that we write about what we most need to learn, and I'm happy to accept that getting along well with other people is the area of my own life I most need to develop. I believe most of us could do a much better job of getting along with each other. The tools are available. We just need to pick them up and use them. Life's too short not to.

NLP is a great way to improve our ability to form, develop, and sustain relationships, even though in origin it's a system for coaching and therapy. These disciplines are fundamentally about people and require very high-quality relationships with clients if they are to be successful. Such fields are, therefore, a good place to look for people skills.

I am surprised more has not been made of the application of NLP to relationships. Perhaps most practitioners are focused on ever more challenging coaching and therapy problems. Maybe it's only obvious to me in retrospect, having come to the subject for other reasons. Whatever the explanation, we're not making as much use of these practical techniques as we could be.

You might be sceptical that you can be systematic with other people and still be human. In fact, an effective approach will help you come across as confident, charismatic, and compassionate if you choose. The idea is to be systematic in how you approach a relationship, not to fit the other person into a process.

The NLP background

In the 1970s, two researchers, Richard Bandler and John Grinder, studied the methods and ideas of a number of leaders in their fields, all working with people in various ways. These included Fritz Perls, Gregory Bateson, Milton Erickson, Virginia Satir, Frank Farrelly, and others. At first sight, the researchers' subjects were doing disparate things to achieve their results, but at a deeper level, they were all operating in a similar way that, once abstracted, formed the foundation of what later became known as NLP. The title itself is best not taken too seriously. It's an inadequate label for both the deeply human nature of the subject and the genius of the originators in articulating it. The subject eludes both precise and concise definition. Thinking of it as practical psychology, however, is a good starting point.

Some awareness of origins is helpful: Fritz Perls (1893–1970) developed Gestalt therapy. Milton Erickson (1901–80) was a groundbreaking psychotherapist and hypnotherapist. Virginia Satir (1916–88) approached families with a problem person as a complete system, regarding the difficult individual as more of a symptom than a cause—groundbreaking at the time. (Extrapolating Satir's work to organisations doesn't seem so fanciful.) Frank Farrelly developed the approach of Provocative Therapy, which among other things, involves playing out the likely consequences of a client's choices in a simultaneously robust, humorous, and loving way, all to good effect. NLP also draws on Noam Chomsky's work in linguistics, Alfred Korzybski's work in semantics, and Gregory Bateson's work in anthropology.

NLP emphasises what to do to achieve useful results, in particular by studying what works well and identifying "the difference that makes the difference" or "the secret of excellence."

NLP studies the structure of subjective experience as opposed to the factual, logical, "objective" dimension with which we are familiar. Subjective experiences, emotions, and unconscious patterns are, of course, central to relationships.

NLP is about developing flexibility and achieving success, and it is ultimately a way of life and a process of a continuing education and curiosity—not something to be turned on and off, but a set of attitudes and skills to be used all the time.

Reactions to the mention of NLP range from "Never heard of it," to "Isn't it manipulative?" to "What a fantastic set of skills." It raises eyebrows for three reasons: first, its relative disinterest in the science of why our minds do what they do (it's more concerned with what works); second, its power and the perception that it can be used to manipulate; and third, its jargon. The name itself seems to imply something devised and technological, which has inhibited our adoption of a powerful body of knowledge and given us a reason to place the whole topic at a distance and miss its relevance.

Some perceive the power as somehow sinister, either through fear of the unknown or witnessing someone manipulating others into doing things that are not in their best interests. Not all who have trained in NLP are good models. NLP itself isn't manipulative. It's what we do with it—what our intention is—that determines whether or not the result is manipulation.

Some say they do not want anything to do with NLP, but they are missing out on understanding how we function as human beings. Sometimes those in positions of authority decide it's not for their organisations, which is a shame when they and their people could benefit so much.

These doubts are unfortunate and ultimately misplaced because NLP can be used to achieve tremendous change both within ourselves and with other people, and there is no obvious alternative source of practical, actionable information in this area. Although the term is often taken to mean a set of skills, in fact it's a reference to the patterns or habits by which we organise our lives. We're all running neuro-linguistic programming all the time, whether we know it or not, so it's not so much outside ourselves waiting to be learned as inside waiting to be understood. If NLP didn't exist, we'd end up discovering it again and calling it something else.

Can we use NLP in relationships?

Yes. Moreover, I don't know any other way to structure the subjective experiences that naturally arise between one person and another. We can improve our handling of relationships by adopting a systematic approach based on fundamental elements of NLP and other aspects of practical psychology, even though the situations themselves may still hold challenges.

A number of well-known authors address relationships, but often don't include any "how-to" information to help you do something different—and we need to do more than just read their books if we are to acquire the skills the authors describe. The great advantage of NLP is that it is practical and puts you in charge with things you can actually do to make a difference.

This book draws on NLP in two ways: The first is directly through the relevance of specific concepts, techniques, and principles; the second is indirectly through the habit of studying and replicating excellence, such as approaches used by individuals who excel in relationships and interpersonal skills, but which may not be NLP ideas in themselves.

Newcomers to NLP often comment that they are not sure how to apply it to their everyday lives. Like many topics, it can be laden with terminology. Here, we will use the straightforward language the subject deserves.

Steps in a circle

I have organised the material we cover into 12 Steps. A book requires its contents to be organised in a sequence, yet there is truly no linear structure to relationship skills, so we proceed through the topics in the order in which they are most easily conveyed. Later ones build on those that have gone before in the manner of a journey. We start with behaviours and attitudes; move on to skills to do with thinking styles, communication, and personality; then proceed to work with more deeply-held things such as values, beliefs, and our sense of identity. All the while, we're building toward the profound and lasting insights that will transform our relationships with other people. We arrive in the end at the topic that brings together and transcends all that has gone before: love. To excel at relationships, even business ones, we must develop both our understanding of what that word means and our ability to go about our daily lives in a way that enriches rather than diminishes both ourselves and others. Arriving at the end of the 12 Steps, in a sense, brings us back to the beginning, ready to focus on other people with new strength and new insight—hence the circular aspect.

My intention is a journey that is at once practical and reflective, concrete and spiritual, robust and loving, challenging and reassuring, and above all, useful. Along the way, we cover such details as the questioning word that you're really better to avoid, a set of principles that are all you need to know to have the right attitude for relationships, the one unmet need that tends to dominate our lives (which might not be what you think!), and lots more besides.

In everyday life, all aspects of our subject are happening in parallel all the time, and they also mesh with each other—every topic supports every other topic, so we won't get hung up on the order. Steps in a circular structure or slices of a cake are appropriate models. In a face-to-face workshop, we would work with several topics at the same time. There is no beginning and no end, no linear path through relationship skills. They're all in use simultaneously and you'll never finish with them. Once learned, you won't want to be without them.

In fact, you'll wish you'd known years ago. Revisit all the topics after you have been using them for a while. As you do, your understanding of each one will be enhanced by your knowledge of the others. This is intended to be a book you return to for more insight into how you may approach your relationships more effectively.

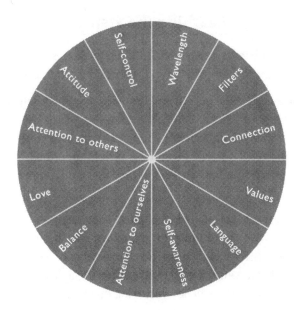

The 12 Steps by no means cover every possible skill for building and nurturing relationships (or every aspect of NLP), but if you learn, practise, and use them all—or even some of them—they will give you success with all kinds of people in your life.

When it comes time to act, you have to oversimplify. Frank Farrelly

It doesn't matter whether the Steps are complete because they are enough to:

- Propel you from the majority who get by at best with other people to the few whose skills are seen as exceptional
- Eliminate interpersonal skills as an issue in your life
- Start you off on your own learning and discovery

When you learn even half of what's in this book, you will be more than capable of continuing on your own.

Learning the Steps

Learning by experience is much more educational than learning consciously. You have to learn to swim in the water. Milton Erickson

We'll look at each Step in turn and then how to apply them all in typical situations. There is an issue of depth: We need to go deep enough into each topic to be sure that you experience enough to convince you we're on solid ground and can build upwards from these firm foundations. We're looking for the learning that has, for you, that undeniable truth from which no one can shake you.

Your own experience will be the most convincing evidence that the approach works. The opportunity to try things out is all around, so the ultimate responsibility for evaluating the effectiveness of each aspect in your life is yours. (Taking the initiative yourself and not being dependent—being "at cause" rather than "effect"—will be a recurring theme.)

Everything in NLP can be directly verified in your own experience or by observing others. Richard Bandler

I have used these skills to rescue and improve my marriage, develop my own business, and organise my life the way I want it. Everything I have included is tried and tested and widely used in other contexts.

What is the worst that can happen when you try out the Steps? Nothing—you don't get the outcome you want and that's about it, and you still have the opportunity to try again. What is the best that can happen? You learn something that makes an immediate difference and convinces you to do more. Have an open mind. Suspend judgment about whether to use a particular skill until after you have learned it. Mixing up evaluating and learning something because you're not sure you like it slows the process. As Sydney Rosen says, "Experiential learning is best done when one is simply experiencing and not examining the experience." By all means, be sceptical afterwards, but from a position of knowledge.

The ideas in the Steps are very powerful, so much so that you must use them with integrity; otherwise, all you'll do is to make undesirable outcomes happen faster.

You may find the things you notice making a difference are simple, shockingly simple. So simple you doubt they're the change you're looking for. Most often, they will be. Avoid missing the answer by looking for something complicated.

Accepting change now

We may need to change ourselves to improve our relationships with other people. We may go through the stages of a familiar process:

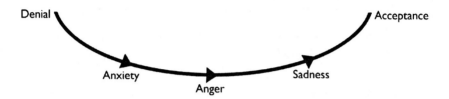

At first, we may deny we need to change, then we become concerned or even angry, then sadness may set in, and finally, we accept the new reality. In the early stages of change, we may feel confused because we have learned something that is inconsistent with our previous beliefs. Confusion is a sign that things are changing and we are making progress. Think of confusion as "the doorway to understanding."

Expect to be challenged by this book. If you weren't, there wouldn't be much point in reading it. You might even find something you disagree with, in which case you'll need to decide whether you know better than me, which is entirely possible, or whether I've highlighted an area you could do with looking at again.

You may have an emotional response to what you learn in some of the exercises, perhaps even a tear or two may come. That's fine. Emotion is "energy in motion;" it shows growth and change is happening. If you suppress emotion, you block change. The learning is where the emotion is, so to grow, accept the discomfort, welcome it even. Something better than what you have at the moment will be the reward.

Similarly, being defensive inhibits the process of feedback on which you are dependent for growth—feedback either from yourself or from other people. Have the courage to welcome it, good and bad. Feedback is precious because it leads to a better future and is hard to come by. Just accept what people say and thank them for it. Being defensive gets in the way and slows down your growth. As Frank Farrelly and Jeff Brandsma write, "Frequently, the significant others in our lives know us far better than we really know ourselves."

What you accept, you go beyond. If you fight it, you are stuck with it. Eckhart Tolle

Doing your homework

The 12 Steps are expressed simply enough, but you will need some practice in their everyday use, very much like learning to ride a bicycle or play a musical instrument. Without practice and a bit of effort, nothing much will change. You must try things out and see what happens, experience the effects. Initially, this will be a conscious process, but as you gain familiarity, you will begin to use the skills unconsciously, in the learning sequence:

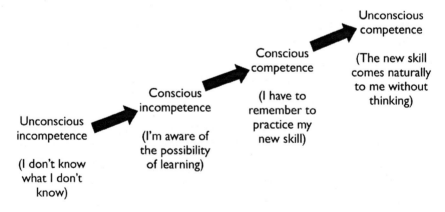

You could read one book after another to gather knowledge about getting along with people, but understanding the information intellectually is not the same as having it in everyday use. Relationships involve emotions and the unconscious mind, so we must complement the rational and conscious approaches that are so familiar to us by learning to notice the emotional side and acknowledging the unconscious processes that have a bearing on what happens. All this takes a little practice.

One way to learn these skills is an interactive workshop, where you try things out and practise with your fellow participants. We are in a different setting here, so I have included "Steps to take" throughout the book. Most are for you to work on yourself. Some ask you to involve friends as partners. The tasks and suggestions are a necessary part of the learning experience. The great thing is, unlike most other subjects, you can learn "on the job" by observing and trying things out as you go about your business. Many of the Steps to take can be worked on during your normal day. No equipment is necessary and there is no need to contrive a learning exercise. You live in the "lab" all the time. Be curious.

This book is about things you can actually do, or in some cases, stop doing: skills you can start deploying, mistakes you can stop making. Of course, that means you have to take action to get any benefit. Changing the quality of your relationships and thereby the quality of your life does involve a bit of work, but not that much set alongside the success you can achieve.

How long will the Steps take to learn?

Everything will be wonderful in a week, but only in your dreams. What a pity to miss out on all the benefits and growth you could have had because you expected to complete the learning process in a week and without any effort. In reality, changes will start happening as soon as you act on what you read here. Learning just one of the Steps or even part of one will make a difference straightaway, but significant growth is going to take a bit longer. Think in terms of 100 days or three months to improve to a point where those close to you might comment on how you've changed. In the span of a life, that's not so long. You can read a Step a day, no problem, but each needs an accumulation of observation, practice, and experience. Picking an aspect to focus on for a few days works well. Your skills will continue to develop over a year or more. It all begins with the decision you've made to start.

Steps to take

 Sit down in a quiet time and space. To relax, take about five slow deep breaths in through your nose and out through your mouth.

Think of creating exactly the relationships you want with the people you want. Be greedy! Never mind how for the moment. Just think about the end result. Who are the people who come to mind? Where is the setting? When is this happening?

Picture the scene. Notice from these people's faces that it is clear they value their relationship with you. What does it feel like to have this success? What is the emotion? What is the physical sensation that goes with the feeling? What are you hearing? What do you say to yourself as you realise you can establish effective relationships easily?

Take these motivational images, feelings, and self-talk with you as you continue.

You will find this easier if you close your eyes for the exercise after you have read these directions. Take some minutes over this.

A systematic approach

In summary

- We can have a systematic approach to relationship skills using NLP as the basis.

- Learning by doing and practice is essential.

- You can evaluate the effectiveness of the 12 Steps for yourself.

- You need to allow time for progress—not all fixes are quick.

- Revisiting the Steps from time to time will help your learning.

- You will only succeed if you act with integrity.

- The 12 Steps are enough.

Relating to you

- What will it be like when you create the relationships you want?

- What's the biggest learning you have taken from this chapter?

Step 1: Attention to others

Shifting your focus

Before *You may:*	**After** *You will:*
✘ Fail to listen properly	✔ Be a good listener
✘ Let your attention wander	✔ Focus on other people
✘ Neglect others' needs	✔ Seem interested and attentive
✘ Seem needy yourself	✔ Feel in control
✘ Come across as arrogant	✔ Seem assured, resourceful, and at ease with yourself
✘ Cut across the themes others want to follow	✔ Get to know people quickly
✘ Talk down to people	✔ Create the opportunity to establish rapport
✘ Promote yourself when you don't need to	✔ Find common ground
✘ Display intelligence when it's not in question	✔ Show respect
✘ Be seen as having a big ego	✔ Have a calming influence
✘ Act the victim	✔ Find that other people tell you everything you need to know
	✔ Achieve win-win outcomes
	✔ Have a common touch

Step 1: Attention to others

You can get whatever you want in life if you help enough other people get what they want. Zig Ziglar

Looking out for yourself takes you so far; to go further, you need to focus on other people. We're off balance, most of us—off balance in focusing on ourselves, talking about our own subjects, and overlooking others' needs. Shifting our focus onto other people is the single biggest step we can take to transform our ability to build and maintain relationships. Most of us are too caught up looking out for ourselves to attend to other people, and yet adopting a behaviour called "attending to others" is the surest way to get results. As Dale Carnegie makes clear, lasting success comes to those who focus on other people. Attending to others is an old courtesy, too much and too often forgotten. The phrase sums up much of Dale Carnegie's *How to Win Friends and Influence People*, as well as "Seek first to understand; then be understood," the fifth habit in Stephen Covey's *The 7 Habits of Highly Effective People*. Even the Roman poet Publilius Syrus is quoted as saying, "We are interested in others when they are interested in us."

Attending to others is a fundamental part of getting along with people, and some of the most profound changes in our relationships come from adopting this simplest of ideas. Our working lives are full of people thinking only of themselves. No wonder the collective results can be disappointing or worse, and it's almost laughable that we expect our organisations to deliver in these circumstances. You can probably think of people who seem to do well—perhaps very well—while trampling on other people, but in my experience at least, they tend to come undone in the end. Our personal lives can also be blighted by unbalanced attention to one or other partner in a relationship. Much is said about the lack of respect in the modern world, which stems from our focus on ourselves. We have a chance to be different and rise above the level of self-interest. As Dale Carnegie writes: "The world is full of people who are grabbing and self-seeking. So the rare individual who unselfishly tries to serve others has an enormous advantage. He has little competition."

We grow up attending to ourselves, so to make a shift toward a more balanced approach, we need a deliberate effort to move to the opposite extreme. Many of us have a big opportunity to improve our relationships by making this kind of shift.

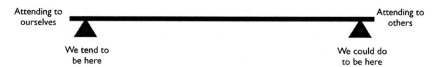

Attending to ourselves — We tend to be here

Attending to others — We could do to be here

You can practise the skill of attending to others so that it is a discipline available when you need it.

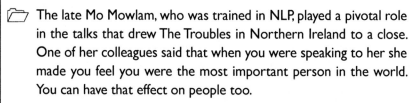

From the example file

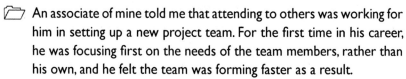

The late Mo Mowlam, who was trained in NLP, played a pivotal role in the talks that drew The Troubles in Northern Ireland to a close. One of her colleagues said that when you were speaking to her she made you feel you were the most important person in the world. You can have that effect on people too.

An associate of mine told me that attending to others was working for him in setting up a new project team. For the first time in his career, he was focusing first on the needs of the team members, rather than his own, and he felt the team was forming faster as a result.

I left school and university with a tendency to focus exclusively on what was important for me or my area of responsibility. Although there are some advantages in being oriented that way, eventually my self-absorption got me into trouble: at work because I didn't pay enough attention to what was important for customers, bosses, and others whose support I needed; and at home because I failed to take enough account of the people around me. I didn't realise that to have my needs met, I needed to meet others' needs first.

Steps to take

 Practise shifting the focus of a conversation backward and forward along a line ranging from totally about the other person to totally about you. Have a few practised phrases such as, "That's enough about me. How are you doing?" and "Can I tell you about...?"

By reading newspapers, watching television, and listening to the radio, we are in the habit of letting others decide where we place our attention. These external influences tend to keep us focused on ourselves when, at one time, we might have realised earlier in our lives that this has its drawbacks. Advertising in particular tends to condition us to focus on ourselves, to suit those who want to sell to us.

To take charge of our lives and put relationships first, we need to overturn this conditioning. Try attending to others for a while and see what happens. What have you got to lose? The results you want are probably eluding you anyway.

Where are you now?

You may think you already "attend to others," but have you developed the freedom, confidence, and flexibility to make the necessary choices by:

1. holding your own experiences, opinions, and ideas back and helping other people develop what they have to say;
2. focusing first on ensuring the other's needs are met and only then turning to your own; and
3. choosing to let the other person lead the style of verbal and non-verbal communication?

If one or more of these is unfamiliar to you and you tend to do just the opposite, you could transform your results by changing these traits or developing the flexibility to alter them when you want to.

From the example file

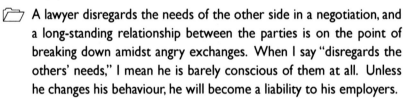 A lawyer disregards the needs of the other side in a negotiation, and a long-standing relationship between the parties is on the point of breaking down amidst angry exchanges. When I say "disregards the others' needs," I mean he is barely conscious of them at all. Unless he changes his behaviour, he will become a liability to his employers.

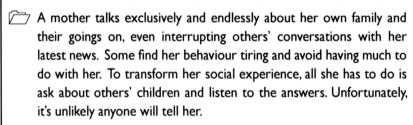 A mother talks exclusively and endlessly about her own family and their goings on, even interrupting others' conversations with her latest news. Some find her behaviour tiring and avoid having much to do with her. To transform her social experience, all she has to do is ask about others' children and listen to the answers. Unfortunately, it's unlikely anyone will tell her.

How to attend to others

A number of specific habits can help us master attending to others. Learning them is easy enough, as they're largely a matter of choice and self-control. For the greatest effect, employ them all, although any one will make a difference on its own:

- Focus on what's important for the other person
- Treat others the way *they* would like to be treated
- Work with their understanding
- Keep your material out of their story
- Listen, and use their words when you speak
- Choose open questions
- Be careful with "why"
- Act as if your needs are already met
- Give others space if that's what they want

Focus on what's important for the other person

You can make more friends in two months by becoming interested in other people than you can in two years by trying to get other people interested in you.
Dale Carnegie

To begin with, keep your own problems, opinions, and ideas to yourself and instead deal only with the other person's content or "stuff." Act for a time as if you have resolved your own problems and had your needs met. Now that's not to say that you forget all about what is important to you. On the contrary, the clearer you are within yourself about your own needs, the better the outcome will be in the end.

Attending to others does not mean being obsequious, fawning, or compliant, and I am not suggesting you should be subservient, but do make the effort to understand the other person and how they see the world. Signal that you respect these things. Be interested rather than interesting. You can still maintain your own point of view and values.

Once you have heard other people out, they will listen to you. In the oft-quoted phrase, "People don't care how much you know until they know how much you care."

From the example file

⌷ Eric has to deal with the unwanted involvement of another manager, Simon, who has a reputation for being abrasive and has just forced his way into a restructuring project of Eric's. Eric, however, knows that what matters to Simon is being seen to achieve cost savings, so a way for Eric to maintain a tolerable relationship with Simon is to play to Simon's interest and let him lead on the cost-saving aspect in return for his support on the rest of Eric's project.

Treat others the way *they* would like to be treated

Most of us were brought up to treat others the way *we* would like to be treated, but it's better to treat others the way *they* would like to be treated. When you want to build a relationship with someone, adapt to them rather than make them adapt to you. You wouldn't say to a boiler: "Give me some heat, and then I'll give you some gas."

Part of this is having regard for the other's self-esteem and in particular, taking care not to cause them to lose face. Be very careful with banter. It's all too easy to puncture someone's ego.

Work with their understanding

If there is any one secret of success, it lies in the ability to get the other person's point of view and see things from that person's angle as well as from your own.
Henry Ford

We all have "models of the world" with which we assess the meaning of new events, using our accumulated analysis of what has happened before. Our models are all different and also pale representations of the world itself. Nevertheless, they are all we have, so if somebody "meets us at our model of the world" as if they are standing in our shoes and seeing things from our point of view, they seem like us and we respond positively to them.

The opposite behaviour is to demand that other people see things our way, which might work if we have authority over them, but not otherwise. One extreme example is expecting others to read our mind and being angry when they fail, saying things such as, "Don't you know why I am upset?" which is a poor strategy for relationship success.

The phrase "meet others at their model of the world" was first used to describe the techniques of Milton Erickson, who would go to great lengths to talk in terms of his client's understanding rather than his own. We can use Erickson's approach in everyday situations.

Steps to take

- When discussing an issue with someone, talk it through in terms of their values, beliefs, and capabilities rather than your own. Work with their understanding rather than yours. Meet them at their model of the world.

- When somebody does or says something that surprises you or seems "out of character," you are overlooking some aspect of their model. Ask yourself: "What would need to be true for them to act the way they did, assuming they had a positive intention for themselves?" Adjust your behaviour to suit.

Keep your material out of their story

When you focus on other people, keep your "content" to yourself, at least at first. You want them to have what you know, but they'll welcome your information when they're ready and not before. The longer you wait, the more interested the other person will be. At first, use your knowledge to ask intelligent and stimulating questions of the speaker.

Hold your information until it's wanted

The right moment to make your point may not come in a particular conversation. You may need to wait until the next time, or the time after that, or perhaps much longer. In organisations, a year or more may pass before you can make the intervention you want to make with any possibility of it being received and acted upon.

All you need to worry about is whether now is the right time. Is the relationship ready for the information? Accept that the time may never be right and that you may never share the information you hoped to impart. If the timing is always wrong, your attempts would be futile anyway. Resist the temptation to speak merely for your own satisfaction.

To accept that you may never tell people about certain things takes a kind of courage, love even. Are you strong enough to keep the burden of your "stuff" away from other people and just to listen instead?

You may be right, but you can choose not to prove it

We often gain nothing by showing we are right and only damage the relationship. We can know we are right without having to show we are right. Often, we can remain silent without conceding. Only rarely are issues settled once and for all. Do you want to be right or do you want to get what you want?

Resist the temptation to compete

Launching into a story of our own when somebody recounts something that has happened to them is a mistake. We can be bursting to express our experience, but will achieve more if we pay attention to the other's story. Resist the temptation to go one better. Let the other person be the focus.

Sometimes we believe we need to promote ourselves. More often than we realise, this can be counterproductive. Beware of the tendency to overdo it. As Dale Carnegie wrote: "Almost all the people you meet feel themselves superior to you in some way, and a sure way to their hearts is to let them realise in some subtle way that you realise their importance and recognise it sincerely."

Steps to take

- Be cautious about giving advice, offering opinions, or telling your story unless asked. Before going ahead, ask yourself if you understand the whole story from the other person's perspective or whether you are driven by your own need to express yourself. Opening with, "If you want my advice," is close to an admission that you expect to be ignored.

- Weigh up the pros and cons of showing you are right about an issue. How would the relationship gain if being right was something you kept to yourself?

- Respect others' themes. Be sensitive to the flow of a conversation and signs that the time is right for a new topic (or not).

- When other people promote themselves or show their intelligence, how does it affect their relationships? What is the learning for you?

- Be alert to signs that you are already accepted by a person or a group and need not sell yourself.

Listen, and use their words when you speak

Relationships work when we listen. As Maria Galenza said: "Most people need a good listening to, not a good talking to." That, of course, translates into an opportunity. The more we listen to people, they more they tell us. Listening well takes effort, practice, and skill, but you can develop your ability easily when you decide to. Limit yourself to asking questions that clarify or explore what the speaker is saying rather than thinking about what you are going to say next, or interrupting—unless that's the only way you'll have a chance to speak.

From the example file

- Andrew is a bit of a charmer and talks rather a lot. He makes initial contact easily, but from time to time says things that seem foolish and undermine his position when he needn't be saying anything at all.

You may have been taught to reflect back what someone says using your own words, and this is often suggested. Reflecting back using the speaker's own words is much more powerful. It takes a little more effort and more attentive listening, but it's easily worth it. The issue is this: If the listener reflects back in his own words, the speaker feels that what was said is distorted and filtered by the listener. Something of the intended meaning is lost. The speaker may feel deflated and diminished. The conversation was all about the speaker, which felt great, and now it's more about the listener, and the speaker feels let down. As Joseph O'Connor and Andrea Lages put it: "People's words reflect their thoughts, and their thoughts represent their reality. So the exact words matter."

Words and how they are said mean different things to different people; it's much better to reflect back using the speakers' words, even if we might not completely understand what they mean. At least we stay true to our goal of attending to others and furthering the relationship. The speaker feels that they have been perfectly understood, and moreover, the listener is sufficiently at ease with themselves that they have no need to bring their own words into the conversation. That makes the listener (you) seem both interested and interesting to the speaker. It's better to "parrot-phrase" than to paraphrase.

Steps to take

- Notice when people reflect back what you say using their own words and compare that with instances where your words are used. How do your feelings compare?

- When you reflect back what somebody else says, try expressing what they said in language you would normally use; on other occasions, try reflecting their own words. Notice the effects these different styles have on the other person. Which is more conducive to a successful relationship?

- Set up an exercise with a friend. Let's say one of you is "Alex" and the other is "Sam." Alex chooses an important subject and speaks on it for, say, two minutes. Sam reflects back some key part of what Alex has said using Sam's own words. Alex then speaks for another two minutes on another important subject. This time Sam reflects back using Alex's own words. Alex compares the two experiences and the feelings he had. Repeat the exercise with Sam speaking and Alex reflecting back. Discuss your conclusions.

Use a speaker's own words to ask questions and develop your understanding of what they are saying. As Tad James and David Shephard advised: "Use their jargon, their preferred terms, even if you think they are using the 'wrong' words. It is what it means to them that matters."

As you listen and interact, match the amount of eye contact others make. As Joseph O'Connor and Andrea Lages said: "Eye contact is neither good nor bad, but people tend to give as much as they feel comfortable receiving, so match what they do. A beady stare will not create rapport, however many authorities say that eye contact is good."

Choose open questions

Who controls a conversation: the speaker or the person asking the questions? Our questions have more impact than the statements we make partly because the other person doesn't challenge what they themselves say in response.

Open questions require more of an answer than just "yes" or "no" and can be used to help the speaker articulate what they want to convey. Asking open questions beginning with "who," "what," "where," "when," "how," and "which," rather than closed ones starting with "Is...," "Do you think that...," or "Could you..." will help us focus on the speaker and keep our own thoughts, experiences, and opinions out of the conversation.

We may like to think we know what another person is thinking or feeling, but the reality is that we have little idea. Any question based on our interpretation— and a closed question would be—will be inaccurate to some degree and will undermine the feeling we want to create that our conversation is all about them. (Closed questions do have their place for confirming information.)

Steps to take

 Notice what happens when you guess what another person is thinking and ask a closed question. How often are you exactly right and how often are you off-target? What is the reaction when you miss the spot? Perhaps you notice the other person stiffen slightly. How do you feel when you are on the receiving end? Better to assume you don't know what another person is thinking and ask an open question instead.

> 👣 Take a bit more time and think of a way to ask open questions instead of closed ones when you seek information.

> 👣 In some conversations, as an experiment, restrict what you say just to asking open questions (avoiding "why" for reasons we'll come to in a minute) and see what happens. Avoid stating your own opinions, relating your own experiences, making suggestions, or asking closed questions. Keep the conversation totally about the other person. See how long you can keep this up. Aim for much more than a few minutes, more like half an hour. You may find this takes a little practice.
>
> After a while, the other person may turn the focus back on you. Accept the shift and take your chance to introduce your information into the relationship, but note the feedback. You perhaps probed too deeply for the level of rapport you had, or conversely, your questions weren't pertinent enough to absorb the other person in their own subject.
>
> You may feel unnatural keeping your information out of a conversation, but that's because your habit is to put yourself forward. The discomfort you may feel is an indication of how much scope you have for change. To cultivate a relationship, be prepared to give the other person the space to express themselves.

> 👣 If you're ever stuck for something to say, ask an open question. It's a safe option.

Using open questions skilfully will help you avoid talking down to someone and help you focus on the needs of the other person rather than on your own. You will also give the impression that your needs are already met.

Be careful with "Why?"

For such a small word, "why" can cause a lot of trouble. It can be used for an open question, but it has at least three drawbacks:

- "Why?" can sound judgmental, especially if we are careless with our tone of voice.
- "Why?" is liable to take the other person back into the past or back into a problem.
- "Why?" gives little direction as to what information we are after.

If you ask "Why?", you give control to the other person and risk losing the thread of the issue. "Why" is a lazy word. In using it, we neglect to indicate what information we want and make the person on the receiving end do the work. They may balk at the blank canvas in front of them.

Steps to take

 When you are asked "Why?", notice how you feel—this is a good indication of others' experience. On occasion, unpleasant emotions will rise within you—irritation, confusion, and panic even (how should you answer?). Much depends on the tone that the questioner uses.

 Observe others' responses. (An interview on the radio or television is an opportunity.) If the questioner means to challenge and increase the tension, then asking "Why?" will do the job, but how does it affect the relationship? Is the response the kind of information wanted by the questioner, or is it some defensive or retaliatory statement that confuses the issue? What are your feelings as a listener toward the person asking "Why?" Is asking "Why, why, why?" an attractive behaviour?

Some people say they were brought up to ask "Why?" all the time and that it has served them well. "Why?" may well have worked better for them than just making assumptions or asking closed questions, but asking more carefully crafted ones without "Why?" will help them with their relationships. Asking "Why?" is a defensive move, close to "victim" language and better avoided. The habitual "Why?" person risks coming across as abrupt or bewildered or both, and is liable to receive an intemperate response. Just because a word exists doesn't mean that it's a good one to use. Much of the time, you will get away with "Why?"—but it's best to avoid it altogether. It can make you sound like a small child.

Steps to take

 Ask a question beginning with "where," "when," "what," "how," "who," or "which" instead of "why." For example, instead of asking "Why did you do that?", try asking one of these questions:

> "What was your intention in doing that?"
> "What was important to you about that?"
> "What was your reason for doing that?"

This might seem long-winded, but it will not be as time-consuming as the defensive reaction that happens when you alienate people by saying, "Why did you do that?"

 When dealing with someone who overuses "Why?", respond as if they had asked, "What was the reason for...?" That at least will help you remain calm, as will knowing why you feel provoked.

 Rather than asking yourself, "Why do I feel this way?", it's more useful to ask, "How did I come to feel this way?", which explores the process that led to the feeling, rather than reinforcing the feeling itself.

From the example file

Vicky, a director, repeatedly asks "Why?"—which works for her up to a point; however, her colleagues feel threatened and struggle to converse with her effectively. It seems unlikely that she means to have this effect. She would be better to expand her repertoire of questions.

One of her subordinates said: "I recently had to explain part of our management process. There had been a lot of boardroom discussions, and I was finding it difficult to achieve the necessary cultural changes to make the process more dynamic. I hoped the discussion with Vicky would lead to some support. What happened was actually the reverse. As I set out my ideas, I was frequently challenged with 'Why?'—'Why are you doing that?' 'Why is your team doing that?' and so on. I immediately felt defensive, as if both my professionalism and my intelligence were being challenged. It was exhausting. I felt emotionally drained and demotivated. What upset me most was that the 'Why' question didn't just challenge my approach to my job, it also challenged the relationship. It seemed to me that there was no trust.

"Perhaps I had taken the questions too literally and seen them as disapproval of my objective and approach. I realised I had assumed my manager knew the outcome I was seeking. Afterward, I decided that if I thought of the question as 'What outcome will your approach result in?' instead of 'Why are you doing that?', I would feel less challenged and more in control of my response.

"I did find that focusing on what I was trying to achieve rather than on what I was doing made it easier to respond to 'Why?' even though it didn't change the way the questions were asked."

Act as if your needs are already met

We seem to get back from the world what we put out, so if we put out anger, we'll get back anger. If we put out generosity, we'll get back generosity. So we attract more of what we are or what we have. If we put out lack or need, we'll attract lack or need. So to bring fulfilment of your needs, switch from talking about your unmet needs to fulfilling others' unmet needs. Then fulfilling of needs will come back to you because that is what you are putting out. If this principle of getting back what you put out is new to you, you might be sceptical. It is more easily observed than proved. But just think—what if it works for you?

We must become the change we want to see in the world. Mahatma Gandhi

From the example file

 On setting up in business on his own, John found that if he told prospective clients he needed work in order to get his income up, he received few assignments. Once he learned to act as if he was already earning at an acceptable level, work flowed to him much more easily.

Steps to take

 Observe what happens over time and decide for yourself whether people get back what they put out.

 Notice what comes back to you from other people. What does that suggest you are putting out, perhaps unconsciously? What changes would you like to make? If you want to receive something different

from other people, what do you need to put out first?

🦶 Act as if your immediate needs are met, whether they are or not, and address the needs of others. Pay attention to what is important for them. For example, if making a proposal or suggestion, ask if it will work for them, rather than saying it works for you.

🦶 To act as if your needs are already met, even when you think they're anything but, presuppose that you are the solution to the other's problem, you are the right person, or you have what's needed. Don't talk about it, just act as if you are. Then you will avoid the twin dangers of seeming either needy or boastful and will instead convey confidence.

Give others space if that's what they want

The final way of attending to others is *not* attending to them if that's what they prefer. Sometimes they don't want to have to talk to anyone. Look out for the signals. Be ready to let people have space. If others don't want your attention, don't force it on them, even if it means not talking in situations where social conventions suggest that you should. If others would prefer to listen and want you to talk, then talk.

From the example file

📁 I once sat beside someone at a business lunch who wanted just to sit and not talk before the meal began. I respected that and didn't speak to her until later. She thanked me afterwards.

When you attend to others

When you bring together all the ways of attending to others and put them into practice consistently, or even inconsistently, other people will notice a difference, at least unconsciously. They will experience you as being attentive and supportive of them, at the same time as being at ease with yourself. You will seem in balance.

Be aware of just how powerful these behaviours are. In demanding situations, the chances are that you'll want to use them all. At other times, you can be more casual. What we have covered here will rebalance your attention from yourself toward other people. You will still focus on yourself and talk about your story when you have the need and the time is right.

When others assume you are in good shape and they don't ask about your issues, it can mean you seem assured to them. Accept the compliment and the slight isolation that goes with it. Your efforts are working. Don't undo the effect by seeking attention.

Steps to take

- Watch out for opportunities to practise attending to others. For example, whenever you interact with those providing a service, focus on what's important for them in the task of serving you, such as completing the process they are expected to follow. Notice the effect on the interaction and how you feel about it. Where else can you make this shift, and what would be the benefits, especially if more is at stake? Dealing with staff in shops, restaurants, and elsewhere is a great chance to learn. As long as you behave with integrity, you can treat everyday situations as a bit of fun.

- To get great customer service, be a great customer.

- Practise attending to others with a friend. Take turns speaking on a subject of your choice for five minutes. The other person asks open questions and practises attending to the speaker and leaving their own content out of the conversation. The speaker can watch out for closed questions or statements slipping in from the questioner. Notice how you feel as the speaker if that happens. You may have a sense of the subject of the conversation being drawn away from you. Feed this back to the questioner. Swap roles. If a third person is available, one of you can observe and provide feedback.

- Remember to attend to others when you are writing a letter or an email. Cover their interests first.

- Talk less and listen more. If nothing else, you'll be less likely to say the wrong thing. In short, ask good questions and shut up.

As you become proficient in the skills we have covered here, you will notice people who never use any of them, never attend to others. You will either need to accept people talking only about themselves or spend more of your time with people who save some of their attention for you. You will become aware of the consequences or absence of these behaviours.

Have compassion toward those less enlightened than you. Buddhist teaching

Step 1: Attention to others

In summary

- Focus on what's important for the other person.

- Treat others the way *they* would like to be treated.

- Work with their understanding (meet them at their model of the world).

- Keep your material out of their story.
  - Hold your information until it's wanted.
  - You may be right, but you can choose not to prove it.
  - Resist the temptation to compete.
  - Respect others' themes.

- Listen and use the other's words when you speak.

- Choose open questions.

- Be careful with asking "Why?"

- Act as if your needs are already met.

- Give others space if that's what they want.

Relating to you

- Who in your life needs some attending to from you?

- What's the first thing you will do differently after reading this chapter?

Step 2: Attitude

Choosing what to believe

Before *You may:*	**After** *You will:*
✗ Act the victim	✔ Take responsibility
✗ Blame others	✔ See the effect of your communication as something you control
✗ Treat failures of communication as someone else's problem	✔ Seem assured, resourceful, and at ease with yourself
✗ Be seen as a critic	✔ Be attractive to other people
✗ Be stuck in problems	✔ Have a calming influence
✗ Give up easily	✔ Be solution-oriented
✗ Expect people to see things your way	✔ Accept difference
✗ Be surprised when what happens isn't what you expect	✔ Respect others' viewpoints
✗ Disregard the interdependence of mind and body	✔ Look behind the behaviour you notice
✗ Dwell on difficulties and in so doing make them bigger	✔ Increase your flexibility
	✔ Be open to change and learning
	✔ Focus on what you want rather than what you don't want

Step 2: Attitude

There is nothing either good or bad, but thinking makes it so.
William Shakespeare (*Hamlet* Act II, Scene 2)

Of all the things we can do to make our relationships flow, sorting out our choice of attitude is one of the most important. What exactly do we mean by "attitude?" An attitude is a combination of the beliefs, values, strategies, and behaviours we adopt—a part we play. We take an attitude of some kind all the time, which may or may not attract comment.

To manage each and every one of our attitudes to situations as if they were new and separate would be difficult indeed, but NLP offers a system that pretty much does the whole job with 12 principles or "presuppositions." Each involves choosing to act as if certain things are true about the world and the people in it. Any one of these principles on its own can transform your results in life.

Richard Bandler and John Grinder gathered the presuppositions from their study of world-leading achievers in various fields, particularly those working with people in challenging situations, such as Virginia Satir and Milton Erickson, who approached their work with attitudes that helped them achieve great results over time. They presupposed certain things were true. If you act as if the presuppositions are true, they will work for you as well. Others will tend to play along, and you will find them to be true in your experience.

The presuppositions empower you in relating to people and help you get more of what you want and less of what you don't want. Whether they are objectively true or not is beside the point. They are a set of principles to live by and involve taking responsibility for what happens in your relationships, rather than being a victim. A fundamental principle of NLP is recognising that you can be in charge of what happens or your response to it, rather than being at the mercy of events. So aim to be at "cause" rather than at "effect." Or as Stephen Covey says, "Work on things you have control over; on your 'Circle of Influence' rather than your 'Circle of Concern.'" When you do, your Circle of Influence will grow.

The presuppositions also help you manage your emotions because you become more resourceful, less judgmental, and more accepting of what happens. The beliefs inherent in the presuppositions influence your behaviour and, in effect, tidy up your attitude.

The power of NLP comes from living the presuppositions as much as from clever coaching techniques. The principles help you come across as mature and calm, which others find appealing and attractive; however, with that attractiveness does come power and, therefore, responsibility.

Living the presuppositions has improved my results, and I am aware of the power the principles bring. With that has come a sense of responsibility and confidence. I no longer need to prove certain things to myself, and so I have no need to impose on other people. It's enough to know what I could achieve with that power without actually having to achieve it. Learning the presuppositions has helped me make my behaviour acceptable so that I can relax with other people in the knowledge that I know how to conduct myself in a suitable way.

Here, we'll adopt a set of 12 presuppositions under loose headings appropriate to the subject of relationships: understanding, flexibility, behaviour, choice, and learning and discovery.

Understanding

The map is not the territory

In 1931, Alfred Korzybski first expressed this principle: Our "map" or mental model of the world is only that—our model of the world, not the world itself (the "territory") and not the same as anyone else's set of beliefs about how the world works and what particular things mean. To relate successfully to you, I must respect your unique model of the world and recognise it as different from mine whether I approve of it or not. The more differently we see the world, the more challenging it may be for me to respect your map, but nevertheless, that's what I must do. Moreover, our models largely reside in our unconscious minds and so differences may come to light at unexpected times.

Problems start if we behave as if our map of the world is complete and the same as everyone else's. To have such a perfect model, we would need to have experienced everything that every person in the world has ever experienced and know how everything in the world works, which is a ridiculous idea.

Interacting with other cultures can reveal to us that aspects of ourselves we thought were just part of being a human being are actually part of an imprint—our map—and therefore both something learned and something we can change if we choose. As Stephen Covey says, "Each of us tends to think we see things as they are, that we are objective. But this is not the case. We see the world, not as it is, but as we are—or, as we are conditioned to see it."

Steps to take

- Respect other people's models of the world and understand those parts of their map that affect their relationship with you.

- If others use a particular scheme for describing the world, then use the same model when talking to them. If members of an organisation use the 24-hour clock, for example, use the same system when you speak to them.

- If you want others to respond in a different way in the future, find ways to help them develop their model of the world, so that they place a new interpretation on information they receive. Giving them a reason for a course of action will be more effective than trying to change their response directly. This point is particularly obvious with children. To have them behave differently, you need to educate them in some way.

- Avoid the phrase "in the real world." All you're saying is, "in my map of the world." Another person's map is as much "the real world" as yours is (and as little).

He that is good with a hammer tends to think everything is a nail.
Abraham Maslow

The meaning of any communication is indicated by the response it gets

We can decide that we are 100 percent responsible for the effect of our communication or lack of communication. The response we get reflects the meaning that the other person took from what they thought they heard us say and how we said it, interpreted in their model of the world. Is that the meaning we intended or wanted? If not, our communication was defective, and it is up to us to try something different to change the result.

Living by this principle, you will never again say, "You don't understand," "You've missed the point," "You don't get it," "You've misunderstood," or "You're over-reacting." These responses all involve incorrectly blaming the listener or listeners for the failure of *your* communication.

Expecting someone to know what we're thinking or why we're upset, for example, runs counter to this principle. If we haven't said anything at all and the result is confusion, we'll make better progress if we take responsibility and express our views or feelings.

From the example file

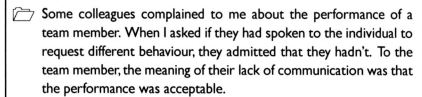 Some colleagues complained to me about the performance of a team member. When I asked if they had spoken to the individual to request different behaviour, they admitted that they hadn't. To the team member, the meaning of their lack of communication was that the performance was acceptable.

I made what I thought was a fairly innocent, if risky, remark to my wife, but judging from the upset it caused, there was more meaning in what I said than I intended. I'd like to say that I took full responsibility for my mistake and avoided blaming her for the "over-reaction," but I regret that wouldn't be true. It wasn't the first occasion and I doubt it'll be the last. Conversational blunders happen. The intent of the presupposition is to own the consequences and do something about them.

Steps to take

Notice how you feel next time someone blames you for the shortcomings of what they've said, using "You've missed the point" or a similar phrase. How will you change what you say and do when you think you haven't been understood?

If you sense someone hasn't understood what you said, explain the point again in a different way. Be aware of signs your message has or has not sunk in.

If a response is not what you expected, take charge of the problem—this is an easy way to gain respect because so few people do it. Say: "Perhaps I wasn't sufficiently clear. Let me explain it another way," or something similar. Develop phrases that you can use when what you said didn't have the effect you expected.

> If you find yourself saying, "So-and-so doesn't get it," or "They don't get it," referring to third parties, you haven't communicated effectively. What are you going to do differently? If they don't get it, you still have work to do. If you are a manager and your staff members "aren't getting it," you need to communicate more and better.

> When you have the feeling that the people you are trying to persuade "just aren't listening," you haven't yet come up with a powerful enough way to communicate with them. Try something else. At times, you may need to be robust, face an intemperate or frosty response, or take risks to elicit the response you want. If your meaning is that something is not acceptable, that's what you'll need to communicate.

Flexibility

Mind and body are parts of the same system; change one and you affect the other

Our bodies are much more involved in thinking, memory, and emotional states than our education might suggest. We are more animal than we may care to believe. For example, we may find walking helps us think through a problem or swimming can induce a meditative state. Musicians find their bodies as much as their minds recall how to play a piece of music. In particular, our unconscious mind is closely linked to our body. It runs it for us, after all.

Emotional states are reflected in physical behaviour and vice versa. We often associate emotions with parts of our body and use language such as "gut feeling," "churning stomach," and "spring in our step." Consciously working with this physiological coding of emotions can be very helpful. When other people's emotional state changes from, say, relaxed to concerned, something changes about their body, such as their posture or breathing. When they discover something new about themselves or a situation, that change often produces a sigh, for example. We can infer what is happening in their minds from what we see in their physical being.

Steps to take

- When you sit down to talk with a group of people, try sitting in a different place from your usual choice and notice the effect on your experience. The physical change affects your mental processes.

- Be alive to the changes in a person's whole being and what these may indicate. You can "read" more than you may have realised.

- Whenever you feel you have run out of mental flexibility, try some physical flexibility, such as a stretching exercise or moving around. Going for a walk when you have a problem to ponder helps your brain work in a different way.

- If a meeting becomes strained, try having everyone move around. Use flexibility in the physical dimension to shift the mental processes. A "time-out" can actually speed up a meeting.

- Use some physical movement as a preparation for a demanding conversation.

- Develop physical flexibility to increase your mental flexibility. Learning T'ai Chi, even at a very simple level, is one effective way of doing this.

The person with the greatest flexibility of thinking and behaviour is likely to have the greatest influence

The more flexibility we have, the more likely we are to hit on an approach that will work. There is no one right way. One size does not fit all. Sometimes, having flexibility can be as easy as giving ourselves permission to do or say something different. The only one stopping us is ourselves. Actors and stage performers give themselves permission to do what may seem extreme things. Which is the act and which is the "real" person—or are both different expressions of the same person? Do great actors have influence? As Robert Dilts says: "The people who are the most effective are the ones who have a map of the world that allows them to perceive the greatest number of available choices and perspectives."

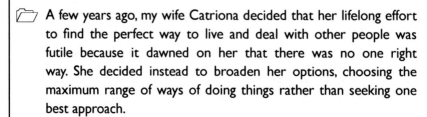

To empower ourselves, we can choose to believe that other people are never difficult, we are merely being inflexible—that there are no difficult employees, only inflexible managers; no difficult customers, only inflexible businesses; no difficult spouses, only inflexible partners; no difficult children, only inflexible parents and teachers. We just need to find the approach that works.

Steps to take

To have more influence, develop more flexibility. Mix with different people. Read things you wouldn't normally read. You'll learn more with people who are different from you than you will with those who are like you.

In a situation involving a number of people, whose lead is being followed? Who has the greatest influence? It must be the person with the greatest flexibility. What is the nature of his or her flexibility? What can you learn from that?

Notice people who are successful in relationships. What is the flexibility they have that is helping them? How can you adopt the same approach?

If we have a range of behaviours or skills we can use (which is a source of influence and strength), we may need to refine our ability to choose which ones to use in different situations. An inappropriate choice may be counter-productive. Skills that work with children may not be the best ones for business colleagues, for example. Using management techniques with your life partner might not be a good idea either (or perhaps it would!). Other cases are more subtle. In my working life, I have several roles, depending on the context: director, manager, mediator, consultant, coach, and trainer. I have at least some of the skills needed for all of these roles, but I have learned through painful experience that using some skills and behaviours that are central to one role, such as the firm leadership of a director, can be a big mistake in a training role, for example. That sounds obvious, but being clear about what works where and avoiding the temptation to import behaviours from other roles takes self-control, especially in a challenging situation. Develop both your flexibility and your ability to make the best choice of behaviour.

Behaviour

It is possible to find a positive intention behind all behaviour

We always act in a way that seeks an outcome we desire at some, perhaps unconscious, level; even, in some cases, if it is bad for us in other ways. Our actions may have consequences that others dislike, but we have an intention that is positive for us. Other people are just the same. If we can identify the positive intention behind their behaviour, we are much more likely to come up with a response that is effective.

If instead we decide to label people's behaviour "bad" or "evil," we disempower ourselves from taking any action to improve the relationship. We trap ourselves in the problem and become a victim. If we look for the positive intention, surmise what it is, or at least assume that there is one, we come up with actions that may meet part or all of their desires in a different way that is acceptable to us.

Commonly, our reaction to this presupposition is to question whether "immoral" or "criminal" behaviour can possibly come from positive intention. Whether behaviour is acceptable or not depends on our values. NLP itself is neutral. The purpose of the presupposition is to look for the underlying intentions that, once found, could be satisfied in a different, benign way. As Robert Dilts says: "It is easier and more productive to respond to the intention rather than the expression of a problematic behaviour."

From the example file

 Looking for the positive intention behind terrorists' actions can help us see things we can do that may change their perspectives enough that they use less extreme, non-violent ways of communicating. For example, the positive intention for some may be to redress the imbalance in power that they perceive between one nation-state and another. Offering fairer ways to share resources might be enough to prompt a change to non-violent means of expression. (Terrorists, of course, are freedom fighters in some models of the world.)

 If children are slow with their homework and seem to require much parental supervision, it could be that they want more attention, especially if, once the homework is finished, they are normally left to their own devices. The parents are rewarding behaviour they don't want. Instead, it's better to promote efficient completion of the homework by engaging in a joint, fun, or interesting activity afterwards. This may take more effort to begin with, but if the insight is right, the approach will solve the problem.

Steps to take

 Next time you notice yourself responding unfavourably to other people's behaviour, ask yourself what their positive intention is. What must you infer to make sense of what they are doing? What would need to be true for them to behave the way they are behaving? How can you best use that knowledge?

 Think about actions your partner or family members take that you dislike. What is the positive intention behind their behaviour? What need are they trying to fulfil (that they see as more important than you do)? You may find it easier to help them achieve their intention than to change it.

The identity of a person is different from the behaviour they demonstrate

People are not their behaviours. People have behaviours, and we believe that they always do the best they can with the resources they have available.
Tad James and Wyatt Woodsmall

The behaviour we observe in another isn't a complete picture of that individual. We know there is much more to people than meets the eye. All we can do is observe their appearance and behaviour, either of which we may not like. If we dismiss them on this basis alone, we risk missing out on a useful relationship. Conversely, we may find a person initially attractive, and then discover that their values are at odds with our own. Hence the old saying: "Don't judge a book by its cover."

From the example file

 Some people find me reserved on first meeting. I don't mean to create that impression and would prefer not to; however, I can say that in the end, these same people have found me to be a dependable and caring friend.

We tend to measure other people by their actions and ourselves by our intentions. They do the same with us, of course.

Steps to take

 What lies behind the behaviour you experience? Who is the whole person behind what you experience directly? How can you adapt your approach?

 How much are you flattering yourself by measuring your intentions rather than your actions, or by being critical of others by focusing on their actions and ignoring their intentions? How would the relationship benefit if you took a realistic, balanced view?

People make the best decisions available to them at the time

People do things that seem a poor choice, but as Richard Bandler and John Grinder put it, "However peculiar their behaviour may appear to us, it makes sense in their model of the world." A better choice in the future can come from enhancing their map so that they have a wider range of options from which to choose. We are more likely to remain resourceful in a tense situation if we remember that we all make the best decisions available to us at the time.

Applying the principle to my own life has been a great comfort. It has allowed me to move on and not be consumed by regret over my mistakes, particularly ones that have affected my marriage and family and can't be reversed. I am not suggesting that you should disregard the consequences of your actions—you know I don't mean that—but once we've done what we've done, it can't be undone, and we can only redress the balance if we move on.

We have a tendency to judge past actions, both our own and others', against the understanding of life we have now, but maybe it isn't helpful to judge our behaviour at 20 against the wisdom available to us at 40. We would do better to accept that we did the best we could at the time, as did everyone else. Our "maps" were different then.

From the example file

 Jackie felt guilty about the lack of attention she paid to her daughter at an earlier age. She cried as she talked about it, but she realised that she had done the best that she could at the time and it only spoiled the present if she dwelled on what she might have done in the past. The guilt she carried was of no benefit to her daughter, and she described it draining out of her body as she realised she could let it go.

Steps to take

 Rather than being critical of others' past mistakes, invest your energies in helping them develop their models of the world and increasing the chances of a better decision next time.

 Think of a time when you did something you wouldn't do now. In what way has your model of the world changed to cause your "best decision" to be different now?

Forgive yourself for things you regret. The chances are that you still feel guilty long after everyone else has forgiven you, if they even remember. You don't serve anyone in the present by being burdened by guilt about the past.

 If you regret something in a relationship, ask yourself how the amount of energy you let the issue consume compares with how much you think the other person is still affected. Store away what you have learned from what happened and let go of your guilt.

Choice

People have everything they need to make whatever changes they choose

We all have the capacity within us to resolve problems and differences, and we may only need a slight change to get us started. (This was an important principle of Milton Erickson's.)

Our choices are not dependent on anyone else. It may seem like they are, but they're not. Even situations in which we feel compelled to do something still involve a choice. Everything we need to make these decisions is already available to us. We have within us whatever we need in order to change, and it need not be difficult or take a long time. We place the greatest limit on what we achieve ourselves. Often, the only one stopping us is us.

I learned that I could choose to be calm. I didn't need anyone else to decide that for me. In fact, no one else could. As Frank Farrelly and Jeff Brandsma write: "Individuals are responsible for their own feelings and behaviours and can at least change behaviour (reorganised perceptions and feelings will follow) by an act of choice or 'will'—if they want to."

Steps to take

 When a relationship problem appears intractable, notice the choices you are making that are preventing a resolution. Acknowledging that you have a choice will help you understand and manage the situation, even if you do decide to stick with your original decision. You can at least tell the other person that you have thought about the issue and, for reasons that are important to you, are making the appropriate choice for you. (This is the subject matter of *The Power of a Positive No* by William Ury.) Or you may decide to make a different choice after all.

 When faced with a problem, recall a time in your life when you had the resources you need now. As Sue Knight suggests, by taking yourself back to that time, you bring those resources into the present.

Energy flows where attention goes

We become what we think about. Earl Nightingale

What we pay conscious attention to determines what our unconscious mind delivers and what will develop between us and other people. So if we focus on something going wrong, it probably will. If we focus on something going well, then that will probably come true as well.

Our unconscious mind has trouble with negatives. For example, what happens if you read: "Don't think of a blue tree?" Most likely you did just that. It's much better to focus on what we do want. What we pay attention to gets bigger.

Of course, we need to think through our problems, but care is needed to channel our energy into what we want rather than what we don't want. I have learned that I can choose what I pay attention to and avoid the things, temptations, and people with whom I may mess up my own life.

If you think you can or if you think you can't, you're probably right. Henry Ford

Steps to take

 When someone talks about what they don't want, divert the energy toward a solution by encouraging them to think about what they do want instead. For example, people commonly say: "I don't want such-and-such to happen." We can make a desirable outcome much more likely by saying something like: "I think we're very clear about what you don't want. What do you want instead?" It's much easier to deliver what someone does want than the absence of what they don't want. This one idea can make a major difference to your effectiveness. Apply it to *your* wants as well.

If we presuppose that we are the solution to someone's problem in a sales situation, our energies will flow into demonstrating that we do in fact have appropriate answers to the customer's needs.

Avoid speaking critically of people who are not present, even inwardly to yourself. "Energy flows where attention goes," so you're likely to create barriers and build up resistance, both with the subject of your criticism and others who hear. Your sentiments work their way back to their subject. Your unconscious mind is also liable to deliver incongruent messages in your body language as you attempt to put on a different front when face-to-face with the person you were talking about. Individuals who hear what you say about someone else wonder what you say about them when they're not present. To set yourself an ideal standard, assume that everything you say (or write) is heard by everybody. In some organisations and families, that can be literally true.

Take great care about where you focus your attention. It grows.

Learning and discovery

There is no such thing as failure, only feedback

At first, we may not achieve the results we hope for with other people. We could see that as failure, but we can also choose to see it as feedback that we have not yet hit on a way that will work. Rather than responding to an unfavourable reaction from someone by abandoning the attempt and blaming them for "stopping us," we can change our approach and move closer to and ultimately achieve the outcome we want. Success with people comes from the ability to accept and act on feedback.

True power is the ability to move from failure to failure with no loss of enthusiasm.
Winston Churchill

(NLP wasn't around in Churchill's time, so he did use the word "failure." Other than that, he did pretty well.) If what you're doing isn't working, use your flexibility to try something else.

Steps to take

 Stay resourceful when what you have tried so far hasn't delivered the outcome you wanted. When things don't work, it's just feedback. Patience may be rewarded.

 What more might you achieve if you try again in a different way, where previously you may have given up?

 If what you were hoping for doesn't happen, interpret that as the absence of success rather than the presence of failure. Many times, other people are not against you. They're just not convinced that they should be for you.

There is a solution to every problem

There is always hope that your life can change because you can always learn new things. Virginia Satir

When difficulties arise, presupposing that there is a way forward will help us arrive at one. In her work with families, Virginia Satir believed that there was a solution to every problem. It was just a question of finding it. Where there is a problem in a relationship, we can resolve it, as long as we are prepared to make the necessary choices. We adapt to the problems we encounter. If we haven't adapted enough in a particular case, the appropriate response is to adapt some more. The problem is not the absence of a solution, but inadequate adaptation by us.

From the example file

📁 A complex commercial dispute involved four parties, all with interrelated issues. At the start of mediation, the problem appeared intractable. Resolution would require subsidiary disputes to be

---

Relationship Mastery

resolved as part of a jigsaw making up the complete package. The mediators' outward confidence that a solution existed was critical to settling the various issues, all to be made binding in a full resolution.

Steps to take

 Act as if your relationships are going to work. There is a way to relate to a person or resolve a problem in a relationship.

If it's possible in the world, then it's possible for me, if only I discover the "how"

If someone else can do a particular thing, then it's resourceful to believe we can learn how to do it, if we study the detail of how that other person is achieving the result. For example, we can learn how to work effectively with particular individuals by studying and copying how others succeed with them.

Skill in anything can look like magic if there is a big enough gap between our level of capability and that of the person we are watching. A conjuror creates an impression of magic, but we can study what they are doing. Skill with people can also look like magic, but again, it's possible to understand what is happening.

From the example file

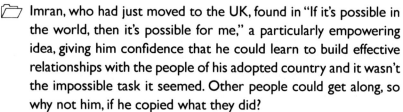

Imran, who had just moved to the UK, found in "If it's possible in the world, then it's possible for me," a particularly empowering idea, giving him confidence that he could learn to build effective relationships with the people of his adopted country and it wasn't the impossible task it seemed. Other people could get along, so why not him, if he copied what they did?

I believe that if it's possible for others to write in a readable way, I ought to be able to learn how to do it too. A school classmate is a well-known writer, and I read some of his work. His standard seemed within reach, which was a particularly helpful exercise in confidence. I studied a number of books on writing style and I hope learned enough to make a decent job of it.

Steps to take

🦶 Think of people who seem particularly effective in relationships. What are they doing to achieve this? Study the details. How can you emulate them?

🦶 If you have difficulties with a particular person, observe someone else who seems to have more success. What are they doing? How can you achieve the same effect?

🦶 If you succeed with some people but not others, what are the things you can learn from your own successes? Perhaps they need adapting to suit your interaction with the people you find challenging.

When we choose our attitude

We've covered a set of 12 empowering principles or "presuppositions" from NLP. Acting in accordance with them will help you manage your attitude and succeed in your relationships. To achieve the benefit, you need to live them at all times, when it's hard as well as when it's easy.

Steps to take

🦶 Digest each presupposition in turn and reflect on how it fits your life. Your interpretation will grow over time. Focus on each one for a few days. How does it empower you to be resourceful with other people?

🦶 Find an opportunity to discuss the principles set out in this chapter with your friends. What do they mean for you individually and collectively?

> 🐾 People who work together regularly can use a shared knowledge of the presuppositions as a general-purpose charter for behaviour, which can prove useful as a reminder for the group from time to time.

The presuppositions involve taking responsibility for our actions and ourselves while avoiding blaming the world and other people for what happens—being at "cause" rather than "effect." If we place blame externally, we disempower ourselves from improving anything. As Debbie Ford said: "It's always easier to blame someone else for what we don't like about our world, but that path is a dead end. There's always pain when you are a victim of circumstance: the pain of desperation and powerlessness."

If we blame others, we have no prospect of improvement in our situation, because we can't change other people. A righteous victim is still a victim. Conversely, if we take responsibility, we can change ourselves. We then have the chance of progress, even though we may feel that we are doing all the work.

Steps to take

🐾 Avoid blaming people. If you witness somebody being blamed for something, what are your feelings toward the person doing the blaming and the person being blamed? How might you modify your own behaviour?

🐾 Avoid blaming circumstances. It's tempting to blame "the traffic" if you're late for a meeting, but you'll come across as weak—a victim. It's better to take responsibility and say, "I didn't allow enough time to get here," which feels very different as you say it. To others, it will seem mature and powerful. Similarly, it's tempting to blame "the IT" for something not being done. You'll make a strong impression if you don't attempt to deflect responsibility, even if it does belong somewhere else.

🐾 Avoid complaining about a problem to those who can do nothing. Complaining just takes you and them out of a resourceful state to no purpose. If something needs to be fixed, deal with it with the people who can act. A typical example of this is criticising the quality of a meal to dinner companions, but not to the provider of the service—this just spoils others' enjoyment. That's being a victim.

- Use "I" or "we" instead of "you" when talking about issues. That way, you take ownership of the problem rather than placing it outside yourself. Instead of saying "You need to...," say "We need to...," unless you really mean to place responsibility on another person.

- Be careful with the use of "one" (and "you" in place of "one"). It's better to identify yourself fully with the point you make by using "I."

In the Applying the Steps chapter, toward the end of the book, we'll say a bit more about the presuppositions. We can learn a lot from them and may ponder them for many years. For just 12 principles, they cover a great deal.

Step 2: Attitude

In summary

Choose a resourceful attitude and "be at cause" with the NLP presuppositions.

Understanding

- The map is not the territory.
- The meaning of any communication is indicated by the response it gets.

Flexibility

- Mind and body are parts of the same system. Change one and you affect the other.
- The person with the greatest flexibility of thinking and behaviour is likely to have the greatest influence.

Behaviour

- It is possible to find a positive intention behind all behaviour.
- The identity of a person is different from the behaviour they demonstrate.
- People make the best decisions available to them at the time.

Choice

- People have all the resources they need to make whatever changes they choose.
- Energy flows where attention goes.

Learning and discovery

- There is no such thing as failure, only feedback.
- There is a solution to every problem.
- If it's possible in the world, then it's possible for me, if only I discover the "how."

Relating to you

- Where will a change in your attitude make a difference for you?
- Which of the 12 presuppositions has the biggest impact on you?

Step 3:
Self-control

Taking charge of yourself might be easier than you think

Before *You may:*	**After** *You will:*
✘ Get anxious and worked up	✔ Be able to control your responses
✘ Let emotions get the better of you	✔ Be accepting of what happens
✘ Look tense	✔ Look relaxed
✘ Be provoked	✔ Have a calming influence
✘ Not perform at your best in meetings and with other people	✔ Listen well
✘ Struggle to focus on any one task when you have too much to do	✔ Deliver to your potential
✘ Not deal well with anger	✔ Be able to focus and hold other pressing matters at bay
	✔ Cope with anger

Step 3: Self-control

If you can keep your head while all around you are losing theirs...
Rudyard Kipling

Of all the things in life we want to control, we have the most difficulty with ourselves. Taking charge of our own state is a lifelong effort for many of us, and key to our success with other people. Some of us seem to grow up with a natural calmness that appears effortless. For others, keeping calm is more of a challenge and something we need to work on. (I am very much in the latter category.)

Working with the NLP presuppositions we covered in Step 2 (Attitude) helps us with our self-control, as we are less likely to feel provoked by what happens in our relationships. However, we can also work at the fundamental level of our mental state, which will help us in our relationships at home, at work, and elsewhere. That's not to say that we should suppress our emotions, but rather to be accepting of them and channel their energy in a useful way.

We can increase our calmness or ability to remain calm in two ways. One particularly effective approach to holding a calm state is to develop the habit of keeping what's called our autonomic nervous system in "relaxation response" or more technically, "parasympathetic nervous arousal." We can do this by controlling our visual awareness and keeping ourselves in peripheral vision (yes, really). We'll look at this perhaps surprising reality in the next section.

The second way to develop calmness is the traditional one of meditation as a route to a mindful and peaceful state. We will look at a simple and straightforward meditation technique in the second half of this chapter.

The habits of peripheral vision and meditation together have brought a state of peacefulness to my life and to my relationships that I didn't have before. Calmness is important in my business of helping people work together in difficult situations, and I have received feedback such as: I "brought a calm to things" and I "calmed everybody down." These comments have meant a lot to me. I would admit, though, that they apply to work situations and I still have room for improvement at home—perhaps a harder place to be peaceful sometimes.

When I was first introduced to the principle of peripheral vision, I didn't realise its importance, and it wasn't until I attended David Shephard's

"Presenting Magically" course that I understood the profound effect. Now, I would say that the habit of peripheral vision is the one technique in this book that will make the most difference to your daily experience of life— just by being more at ease.

Meditation, or even just the remembered experience of meditation, has also helped me. My late mother used to say that I never "just sat and thought about nothing." I ignored her advice, of course. As a younger man, "just sitting" seemed a ridiculous thing to do, but I now understand that she was advocating a process of meditation, although I don't think she would have used the term.

Keeping calm with peripheral vision

We can boost our self-control by working with our visual awareness. Remember we demonstrated in "The need for relationship mastery" that our unconscious mind controls more than we realise? Well, here's another thing our body does that we may not be aware of: It turns out that we can calm down our emotional response to events by using our eyes in a particular (and natural) way—extraordinary, perhaps, but true. If you haven't come across it before, I think you will be amazed at the power of this simple technique, which is a little-known, but easy life skill with a transformational effect.

We can adjust our visual awareness from foveal vision, where we are only aware of what's directly in front of us, through to peripheral vision, where we are aware of everything both in front of us and on either side and even behind us, although we can't see it directly.

These two extremes are associated with different responses of our nervous system. Foveal vision is associated with sympathetic nervous arousal or "stress response," and peripheral vision with parasympathetic nervous arousal or "relaxation response." These are both aspects of the autonomic nervous system, which governs automatic and involuntary action of bodily organs and muscles. Put simply: If we are in peripheral vision, we will remain calm whatever happens, like a martial artist, whereas if we are in foveal vision, we are liable to go into the "fight or flight" response. Foveal vision tenses you up; peripheral vision calms you down.

Being in peripheral vision is the way to be calm and in control of your response to new situations and a vital part of both "learner" state and "trainer" (or "presenter") state, as set out in Tad James and David Shephard's book *Presenting Magically*, where they adapt from Patanjali's *Yoga Sutras* (ca. 600 AD). If we are speaking to an audience, we want to be resourceful and to remain so irrespective of what happens. "Trainer" state (or something like it) is also the state you want for all sorts of other situations, such as meetings, the family dinner table, and the everyday problems that happen in life—anywhere you have an "audience."

So how do we make peripheral vision a habit? First of all, it's likely you will already be in peripheral vision some of the time without being aware of it. We want to become conscious of when we are and when we aren't, so that we can maximise our use of the state.

We can practise being in peripheral vision very easily. For this, you need something to look at comfortably, above eye level—some sort of mark on a wall or a small object.

Steps to take

 First of all, relax, sitting or standing in a comfortable, upright position with both feet on the floor. Make sure your body is lined up vertically and your feet are pointing forward about one foot apart.

Take a deep breath in through your nose and exhale slowly through your mouth.

Focus your attention inward for a moment. (I like to feel my feet on the floor.)

Now look up at the spot on the wall.

Keeping your gaze directed at the spot on the wall, slowly expand your awareness around the spot. Become aware of the other things that you can see in the room. While still looking at the spot on the wall, expand your awareness further so that you notice things on either side of you at the extremes of your physical vision—around 90 degrees right and left. (Our eyes are amazing.) For example, as I write this now, I am aware of a lamp over to my right and a telephone over to my left. (Even though I am typing at a computer, I am in peripheral vision.)

Now expand your awareness even further so that you are aware of what's behind you in the room—things you can't physically see. Take your awareness all around you. You may find it helpful to imagine a ball suspended above and behind your head and expand your awareness to include that.

Once you are aware of everything around you, while still looking at the spot on the wall, you are in peripheral vision. Notice how you feel—possibly a little "spaced out"—with a certain lightness. Objects in the room may appear surprisingly large and any movement may seem exaggerated.

In this state, you are choosing parasympathetic nervous arousal or relaxation response rather than stress response. So long as you stay in peripheral vision, you won't be drawn into a reaction to what happens, but will remain in a relaxed state.

Practise going into peripheral vision so that it becomes something you are aware of and can choose at will. Gradually, you will make a habit of it.

 If you encounter situations with other people that you find stressful and difficult to deal with calmly, get into the habit of going into peripheral vision when you arrive or sit down. (Examples for me would be board meetings at work and the family dinner table with three young children present.) After you've done this a number of times, perhaps about ten, the process will become automatic or "anchored" to the stimulus of arriving or sitting down. When you're in peripheral vision, you'll have an awareness of all the people at the table, even if they're not always in your view. You'll have a heightened awareness of their presence and what they say and do. At the same time, provided that you stay in peripheral vision, you'll be able to choose your response.

To appreciate the opposite effect, notice what happens when you get a fright, like a sudden loud noise. Chances are that your visual awareness narrows as you tense up. Just imagining being taken by surprise is probably enough for you to notice what happens. That's the effect you want to avoid by training yourself to be in peripheral vision.

Peripheral vision makes you feel different, at ease. If this is already your usual habit, you may wonder what all the fuss is about. For others who have had a lifelong tendency to dwell in foveal vision with the tension that goes with it, making peripheral vision your norm is deeply liberating. In peripheral vision, as Tad James and David Shephard say, "You cannot feel any negative feelings. If you do feel them, you are not in it properly."

Calming down with a little meditation

The average human mind is in a state of constant distraction. Rob Nairn

We can also increase our calmness using a simple meditation technique. You may or may not be familiar with meditation. I wasn't until relatively recently. Meditation need not involve trappings or rituals and can be approached in a simple, straightforward, and secular way.

Meditation is one route to a state of mindfulness in which we are fully present in the current moment—"the now"—and ready for anything at any time. Buddhists teach that there is no past and no future in a mindful state. There is no judgment and no grasping. In other words, we are fully in the present and accept things as they are. We neither pull thoughts or things toward us nor push them away. As Rob Nairn says in his book *Diamond Mind*, "Mindfulness can be defined as knowing what is happening while it is happening, no matter what it is."

We can benefit in many ways from working on our mindfulness. As well as making us calm and accepting of what happens in our lives, it also helps us to focus on one thing at a time and improves our ability to listen. Mindfulness makes us both more peaceful and more insightful.

Before we look at a simple approach to meditation, let's follow Eckhard Tolle's suggestion in *The Power of Now* and notice something about the thinking mind:

Steps to take

 In a quiet and relaxed state, become aware of the individual thoughts that arise in your mind as they come and go. Now notice that the part of you that does the noticing is separate from the part of you that does the thinking. If there is a break in your thinking, are you still there? Of course you are. The bit of you that does the conscious thinking isn't your continuing presence. Whatever is the real you, it's not your thinking mind; otherwise, you'd no longer be with us when you're not thinking. The most central part of you—the bit that does the noticing, your awareness—is nearer the real you: your "higher self."

Take a moment to experience this.

Our awareness is different from our consciously thinking mind (and is the part of us that listens and relates to other people). When Descartes wrote in 1637, "I think, therefore I am," he meant that the occurrence of thought proved existence. If we are not thinking, however, that doesn't mean we don't exist. A few moments' observation makes that clear. The thinking part of us is not the being part. As Eckhart Tolle says, "The moment you start watching the thinker, a higher level of consciousness becomes activated," whereas identification with your thinking mind "creates an opaque screen of concepts, labels, images, words, judgments, and definitions that blocks all true relationship."

Through meditation, we associate with our awareness rather than our thinking mind. At any time, thoughts come into our mind, but we can learn to not feed them; instead, just notice them and let them pass. If we don't give the thoughts energy, they fall away on their own.

You can improve your mindfulness and discover the benefits of meditation with a very simple routine you can do anywhere without attracting attention.

Steps to take

 Begin in a physically relaxed state.

Sit in a quiet place without distractions in an upright, comfortable position with your feet flat on the floor and your hands at rest. Place your gaze on a point in front of you a little above eye level—something specific to focus on, like a mark on a wall. You will need some way of knowing what time has passed; glancing at a clock or a watch will do fine for our purposes.

Sit for 20 minutes, looking at your chosen spot and paying attention to your breathing, in and out. Keep your eyes open to avoid falling asleep (which isn't the object of the exercise here).

The aim is to not think about anything, to quiet your mind. However, thoughts will come into your head. Instead of developing them and feeding them energy, notice each thought and let it pass without reacting to it. Typically, some time will go by without you thinking of anything, and your awareness will only be on your breathing. Then you will realise you are thinking about something and that the thought is growing. Instead of pushing the thoughts away harshly, let go of them gently and calmly, and return your awareness to your breathing. You will probably go through this cycle many times, possibly more often at the beginning than at the end of your 20 minutes.

You may find that the thoughts are insistent and demanding of your attention and energy, because of their seeming importance. The gain in this process comes from learning to accept them and let them go. As you do this, the thoughts gradually come less frequently and insistently.

You may find that 20 minutes goes by surprisingly quickly—more quickly than 20 minutes waiting for a train, for example. (Waiting for a train or anything else, by the way, is an opportunity to meditate.)

When the time is up, move on to whatever you intended to do next. Make good use of the calm state you've created for yourself.

Try this as soon as you can. You will easily recoup your investment of time through your increased calmness and focus.

- Whenever you feel panicked by your circumstances, try meditating like this. Chances are, things will seem manageable afterward.

- Regard 20 minutes of meditation as valuable preparation for facing a challenging situation with other people.

This is only the tiniest of introductions to meditation. You can derive many benefits from it, of course, and we are focusing only on calmness for relationships here. Devoting time to meditation may seem like a luxury, but as he led India to independence, Mahatma Gandhi used to say that he meditated for two hours a day, and four hours when he was busy.

When we begin practicing meditation, we find out how distracted and unsettled our minds really are. And what's more, we've been reinforcing the tendency to be unsettled by seeking entertainment for the mind through television, radio, books, and so on, as well as things we drink and eat. We may have avoided letting our minds settle because we fear what would come up when we do. We fear the things that will be uncovered when we stop overlaying them with extraneous distractions. And yet the only route to mindfulness and a peaceful state is through accepting these thoughts. If we continually distract our minds, we have no chance of achieving a peaceful state, although we might achieve a certain numbness.

A continually distracted mind is the opposite of a peaceful mind. In fact, we can train our mind to be unsettled by continually distracting it, or we can train it to be peaceful by avoiding distractions and accepting what comes up within.

One morning in 2008, my wife and I were informed of our son's diagnosis of autism. We had suspected he was on the autistic spectrum, but still the time had come to accept the reality of the challenges to be faced. Against this background, I wondered how I could concentrate on work and interacting with other people. Being distracted from my client's needs wasn't going to help my son, but my initial attempts to focus were futile.

Having been taught the essentials of meditation, I tried meditating in my office for 20 minutes. Thoughts came and went, and it so happened that I wasn't interrupted. After 20 minutes, I found that I was calmer. I could accept the news we had received, concentrate on the work I wanted to do, and speak to the people I needed to speak to. As with many things, I found I didn't need to be an expert or meditate "properly" to benefit. I was fortunate on that occasion to have had the opportunity to take 20 minutes from work, and I realise that will often not be possible. We need to make other opportunities.

The art of mindful listening

As we attempt to listen to someone speaking, we may find our own mind intruding. Calmness will reduce this tendency, but we can also practise "mindful listening," in which we let go of our thoughts as if we were meditating. To listen mindfully:

1. Look at the speaker's face;

2. Hold your awareness on what the speaker is saying; and

3. When you realise your mind has gone off on its own thoughts, notice what they are, and gently and calmly let go of them and return your awareness to the speaker. You will probably do this several times in the course of a conversation.

In other words, the process of mindful listening is like meditating, but you focus on what the other person is saying rather than on your breathing.

During the course in meditation I attended at the Samye Ling monastery, I met a man called Tim who had an impressive ability to listen mindfully and reflect back precisely what others said, up to several sentences at a time.

One lunchtime, I asked Tim a question. Midway into his answer, I happened to break eye contact. Immediately Tim noticed and asked: "Am I answering your question?" He was not being judgmental. He was acting in the Buddhist way of compassion toward those less enlightened than themselves. He was concerned that his response was not meeting my needs. The incident was a profound and humbling lesson on the level of attentiveness that can be achieved and our transparency in such a presence.

Steps to take

 When it's important that you listen to someone carefully, try the art of mindful listening. Hold your gaze on the speaker. Keep your awareness on what they are saying and let whatever thoughts come into your head go past without feeding them. Let them fall away.

Do your thinking only after you have finished listening. You may not respond immediately, but the speaker will be grateful to you for listening to them thoroughly, perhaps more attentively than they have ever been listened to before. It will seem natural that you think before responding. After all, you have a lot to process, having listened to them so carefully.

After listening mindfully, you will find it easier to recall precisely the words the speaker used and that will help you reflect accurately what they said.

When you improve your self-control

An ability to maintain a calm state will help you in your relationships everywhere. Instead of becoming caught up in the emotions, you will be able to keep control of your actions and respond effectively instead.

You will be able to manage your own and others' anger more easily, by not feeding it. Dale Carnegie believed that "you can measure the size of a person by what makes him or her angry." Remember though, that as Virginia Satir said, "Many people are not aware that anger is a necessary human emergency emotion for some," and "It isn't the anger, but the action taken as a result of it that can be destructive." Calmness will reduce the number of "anger emergencies" you have.

Step 3: Self-control

In summary

- Choose peripheral vision and relaxation response to maintain a calm state.

- Use meditation to increase your calmness when you need it, especially when you feel unfocused and under pressure.

- Listen mindfully for maximum attentiveness.

- Use calmness to cope with anger.

Relating to you

- What effect will increased self-control have on your relationships?

- What have you taken away from this chapter?

Step 4: Wavelength

Talking to other people the way they talk to themselves

Before *You may:*	**After** *You will:*
✗ Find it difficult to connect with certain people even though you have things in common	✔ Understand why you sometimes just seem to "click" or "see eye-to-eye" with someone
✗ Be unaware of visual, auditory, and kinaesthetic (VAK) preferences and their importance	✔ Understand VAK thinking styles
✗ Be manipulated by people who are familiar with the VAK domain	✔ Discern your own and others' VAK preferences
✗ Use language lacking in sensory richness	✔ Talk to people in ways that suit them and are accepted easily
✗ Lose people with too much business or formal language	✔ Be able to flavour your written communication to suit your audience
✗ Be unaware how much your life is coloured and shaped by your VAK preferences	✔ Know how VAK preferences reflect your physical being and vice versa
	✔ Understand the implications of VAK preferences in relationships and how to allow for them

Step 4: Wavelength

Stop thinking and come to your senses. Fritz Perls

Ever wonder why you sometimes just can't seem to connect with certain people even though you have a lot in common with them? Or why they just don't seem to be on the same wavelength? In this chapter, we'll look at one of the reasons that this could be and what you can do about it. We'll also see that our lives can be determined by this factor in ways we probably don't realise.

We have individual preferences of visual, auditory, or kinaesthetic (VAK) thinking relating to sight, sound, or touch and feeling respectively, and these are much more than an intellectual curiosity. Some of us also have a liking for internal dialogue, the "auditory-digital" channel (A-D). Our habitual preferences among these alternatives amount to an unconscious lifestyle choice affecting our whole being. Our body, posture, breathing, voice, and words all reflect the relative strength of these "representational systems" within us. Our relationships are also coloured by our own and others' preferences. As Tad James and David Shephard said: "The more we learn of these distinctions, the more we realise how fundamentally different people really are."

From the example file

📁 Alice is slim and dresses fashionably. She walks quickly and moves in a crisp way. She is talkative and has a relatively high voice, which seems to originate in her upper body. She comes across as slightly brittle and perhaps aloof. You are aware of the space around her. She rarely talks about her feelings.

Alice has a strong visual preference.

📁 Steve speaks in a deep voice in a slow and measured way. He is very calm. He breathes deeply. He may take a little time to answer a question, drawing breath before he does so. When talking about his feelings, he is straightforward. His presence is reassuring.

Steve is kinaesthetic.

📁 Ian tilts his head to listen. He can be distracted by sound. His eyes move to the side when he thinks. You are aware of his voice.

Ian has a strong auditory channel.

> 📁 Jack is tall and slim and seems ever so slightly robotic in his manner. He speaks in technical-sounding language in a clipped way, and it can be hard to stay focused on what he is saying.
>
> Jack has an A-D preference.

In relating to people, we want to tune in to their preferences to find their wavelength.

Systems for thinking

Our experience of the world around us is determined by the information we receive through our senses: sight, hearing, touch, smell, and taste. We have a complete internal representational system in our mind associated with each sense to process and recall this information and to create imagined versions of it internally.

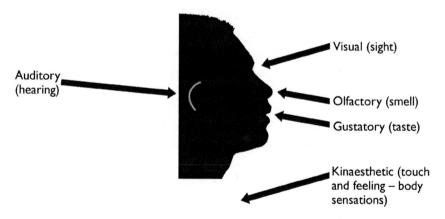

We use these representational systems to do even ordinary things such as walking and speaking, and our actions are made up of sequences coded in the five systems or thinking styles. The visual, auditory, and kinaesthetic channels are the most important to relationships. ("Representational systems" is the proper term, but we will refer to "thinking styles," "channels," and "domains" to mean the same thing.)

These VAK domains are reflected in the way we think and communicate at any given time. We may switch between these channels frequently, using any one for as little as fractions of a second or perhaps many seconds or even minutes. We all use each of these different thinking styles to some extent, but we have individual preferences, partly depending on the context. So for example, some of us think mainly with images and colours (let's call that group "visuals"); others are comfortable with feelings and touch ("kinaesthetics"); and still others concentrate on sounds ("auditories"). For the most part, we are not aware of our preferences or what channel we are using at any particular time.

The relative predominance of visual, auditory and kinaesthetic preferences in the population as a whole is something like:

> 70% Visual
> 20% Kinaesthetic
> 10% Auditory

The precise figures vary depending on the backgrounds of the surveyed group. Visual preference, however, is consistently the most common and often in a majority. Kinaesthetic preference is usually second, with auditory third. One consequence is that our world is rather tailored to visual preference people, and the rest of us could claim to be discriminated against. Many communicators unknowingly assume that their audience is just as visual as they are. All sorts of other disconnects are possible: Unless you're auditory preference, you may not realise how distracting noise can be. On the other hand, kinaesthetic and auditory people may not realise just how much the visuals need to see a picture of some sort. Kinaesthetics may find auditory and visual people insensitive. Visuals notice that auditories break eye contact. Auditory people complain that kinaesthetics don't listen, and so on.

Auditory-digital thinking

We have a fourth thinking style, which is not associated with any of the senses—"auditory-digital" or A-D for short. A-D thinking is "self-talk" or the internal dialogue with which we think things through using language. Training in professional and business disciplines with a predominance of written material tends to lead to frequent use of abstract, A-D thinking, writing, and speech from which the sensory components have largely been filtered out—a preference for A-D.

Even if someone has an A-D preference, one of the other representational systems will be a close second, because they need to have a way of gathering information from their environment in the first place.

In many businesses and organisations, the spoken and written word reflects A-D preference almost to the exclusion of the other three sensory-specific representational systems, partly because professional people have been trained to avoid the emotional dimension, to be logical and analytical instead. However, we find it hard to concentrate on information presented in A-D form and are often left unmoved by it. The visuals are still waiting to "see the picture," the auditories are waiting "to hear the argument," and the kinaesthetics are waiting for some feelings about what is being said. The result can be a lack of motivation to act.

The advantage of working in specific sensory channels is that we connect with the mind of the listener at a deeper, unconscious, emotional level, which results in a much more powerful response. In contrast, as listeners, we need to process A-D information consciously, and because we have to think—which we may not be willing or able to do at the time—the experience is more taxing.

Steps to take

 Think of a conversation you had recently. You will be able to recall something of the scene, how the other person sounded, how you felt, and what you said. These are the visual, auditory, kinaesthetic, and auditory-digital components of your experience. The one you thought of first might suggest your preferred channel.

Representational systems together

With another person, the match or mismatch in our preferences—visual, auditory, kinaesthetic, and auditory-digital—will affect how well we get along. This may be a familiar idea to you: Certain people respond well to visual input like pictures, for instance, but I wonder if you realise just how dominant this effect is.

When people see "eye-to-eye" or "hit it off," they may be well matched in their preferred representational systems—both visual, for example. Conversely, if they "pass each other by," they may be mismatched—one visual and the other kinaesthetic perhaps.

If you happen to be well matched with another person, you will experience a sense of easy communication and will establish rapport quickly. Conversely, if you are mismatched, you are likely to feel not quite at ease and may struggle to achieve rapport. That will have consequences for you. For example, in a business situation, mismatched channels are likely to make it hard for you to close a sale. At home, the result of different preferences can be years of misunderstandings.

From the example file

 A colleague who has a strong visual channel related easily to a client who also is highly visual, whereas my relationship with the same person needed effort. In contrast, I had easy, effortless interactions with the client's deputy, who like me had a mixture of auditory and kinaesthetic preference.

Later, the client asked my colleague to undertake an additional assignment, while I continued the main project with her deputy. The new working arrangements aligned with the VAK preferences of the individuals involved and that was possibly the only reason for the request.

Meanwhile, the client realised difficulties she experienced in relating to her deputy were explained by the mismatch in their VAK preferences.

So are we helpless before all this? No, for two reasons: (1) We can figure out what our own and others' thinking style preferences are, and (2) we can learn to vary our own use of the different channels to tune in to the person we are dealing with.

Discerning preferred thinking styles

We reveal our preferred representational systems to others in many different ways, including:

- The words we use
- The way we move our eyes

- The origin of our voice
- Our breathing
- Our body shape
- The way we move
- Our posture

We can discern others' preferences (and our own) by paying attention to some or all of these indicators. The sheer number of ways of discerning these preferences indicates just how fundamental they are and how much they regulate our lives. Strongly visual, auditory, kinaesthetic, or auditory-digital people are so different in character that they're like different breeds.

The words we use

We use words that reflect the representational system we are thinking with at the time, so a predominately visual person, or someone thinking visually, will use words and phrases that relate to seeing, light, and colour. Individuals with an auditory preference will use words and phrases associated with sound and listening. Kinaesthetic preference involves movement and sensation or words that describe feelings or emotions. A-D thinking produces words that relate to analysis, logic, and knowledge.

Here are some examples of words and phrases that suggest use of a particular representational system:

Visual

I see	illuminate	watch
vision	clear	frame
look at the big picture	reflect	vivid
focus	scene	shine
perspective	image	shed light
colourful	notice	obscure
bright	highlight	show
look	flash	glance
insight	blur	darken
outlook	illustrate	staring us in the face
overview	enlighten	appear
visualise	horizon	mirror

Auditory

tell	roar	state
tune	pronounce	silence
talk	sound	remark
rhyme	speechless	utter
echo	quarrel	propose
whistle	say	quiet
audible	argue	mention
voice	question	loud
hear what you say	listen	overtone
rings a bell	music to my ears	noise
harmonious	playing our tune	moan
deaf	hear	ping

Kinaesthetic—movement and sensation

feel	grasp	soft
touch	get a handle on	hard
wrap arms around	grind down	hit the spot
cool	get hold of	rush
sweat	drive	firm up
shape	pressure	seize
grab	walk	blunt
stuck	impact	touch
crush	swallow	warm

Kinaesthetic—emotions

wound up	upset	lonely
embarrassed	peaceful	terrorised
disgusted	happy	affectionate
stressful	fed up	nervous
calm	inspired	grateful
annoyed	sore	anxious
horrified	depressed	relaxed
passionate	bored	tired
frustrated	angry	relieved

Relationship Mastery

Auditory-digital

statistically speaking	know	understand
reasonable	logical	make sense
procedure	principle	typical
systematic	variable	framework
learning	idea	specific
knowledge	model	theory
meaning	obvious	think
integrated	transition	experience
excellent	special	interactive
random	concept	application

The typical NLP textbook lists words and phrases exclusively against each representational system, as above, but we can be a little more subtle than that. Some words have a role in more than one representational system, depending on the meaning that a particular person takes from them. The following could be interpreted as visual or kinaesthetic, for example:

glow	radiate	expand
scan	paint	foggy
draw	lighten	reveal

Other words could be auditory or kinaesthetic, depending on whether we associate them with a sound or with a feeling or physical sensation:

rebuff	scratch	pitch
snap	beat	articulate
squeak	buzz	resonate
rhythm	click	divulge

Visual and auditory words and phrases are also possible. One example, suggesting either the sight of something being written or something being spoken out loud, is "spell out."

A few words could be associated with any of the visual, auditory, and kinaesthetic representational systems—"wavelength" and "vague," for example.

Where words fit more than one category, we are likely to see them as aligned with our preference, so visual people tend to notice visual words. Words that fit more than one representational system are useful because they connect with more people. "Being on the same wavelength" is a powerful phrase for that reason. Such words, however, can also lead to misunderstandings because those with different preferences will interpret them in very different ways and potentially have very different responses. For example, if you say "draw," meaning to create an image, another person may get a feeling (of holding a pencil) or a sound (of pencil on paper).

If you have a strong kinaesthetic preference, you may look at some of the words I have listed as visual, for example, and think they're kinaesthetic rather than visual. For instance, "frame" may bring to mind the physical action of putting a frame around something rather than seeing a frame around an image. Therein lies the potential for misunderstanding. You say "frame," thinking of the physical activity and the touch of the object, while the visual person sees a picture with a frame around it. You are speaking a different language.

You may well disagree with my allocation of words to categories or be surprised by some of them. In a way, that's the point. Mostly, we're not aware of how we interpret these words, the possible effect of using them, or how that can be quite different depending on whom we are talking to. The opportunity is to be mindful of that.

The specific categorisation of words isn't that important. It's the principles that matter. You're aiming to notice the kind of words that others prefer. Once you know, you can use the same style of words when you communicate with them. You're then talking to them the way they talk to themselves.

My VAK preferences are kinaesthetic and auditory, so the stretch for me is to add in more visual references. I keep that in mind when I write, as I am liable to use more kinaesthetic and auditory wording than might suit the typical visual reader.

Steps to take

 Pay attention to the words people use and see if you can figure out their preferences for VAK and A-D thinking.

 Look over emails or letters you have received and see what you can discern about the authors' preferred representational systems from the words they use. Match their preference when you write to them and see what effect that has.

Study some text with a friend or a group of friends and see if you interpret words in the same way. You may find that your friends notice different words from you, which would indicate something about their preferences.

Look over your own writing and see if your preferences are apparent. How might you change the words you use to increase the chances of matching other people?

From the example file

Here's an example, an email that reveals a kinaesthetic preference (words and phrases in bold):

"Good to **catch** up the other day. I am pleased you are **feeling** much more confident about how things are going to go. It's such a **drag** when people slow things down by **mucking up** the works. I know I feel down when unnecessary **obstacles** get **put** in my way. Anyway, I'm sure it's **sorted** now.

Just to let you know, I've **re-arranged** my schedule and made a **bit of space** so that we can **bring everybody together**. It'll be great to see them all again. It's been a long time and I'm sure we'll have a great night."

There's one visual word—"see."

The next one is noticeably auditory (in bold). Bear in mind the author has just read my email, which "sounds fine" to her:

"Hi David,

This **sounds** fine. We haven't had a chance yet to sit down and look at the appraisals etc.; however, I am hoping to organise that for next week. The behaviours should be on the Intranet by the end of this week, and I am currently **talking** to our marketing department about the booklets & A4 laminates (waiting on costs coming back). So everything is kind of on track!

I will give you a **shout** if I need help."

Kinaesthetic is in there too—"sit down," "coming back," and "on track." Just one visual—"look at."

The way we move our eyes

We're probably well aware that we move our eyes as we think and speak and that we break eye contact from time to time. We may not know that there are pre-determined patterns to this and that the representational system we are using at any given moment can be inferred from the particular direction in which we move our eyes.

If our eyes move upwards, we are thinking visually. Up to our left indicates a remembered image, whereas up to our right indicates a created picture. If we think about sounds in the auditory channel, our eyes move horizontally level with our ears. If we are remembering what somebody said, our eyes move to our left; if we are hearing what we might say in our head, then our eyes move to the right. If we are thinking about feelings and sensations, our eyes move down and to the right. Completing the set, down to the left is associated with internal dialogue, self-talk, or A-D thinking. The following diagram shows the directions of eye movement for a "normally organised" person as you look at them. Visual can also be straight ahead, slightly raised, and defocused.

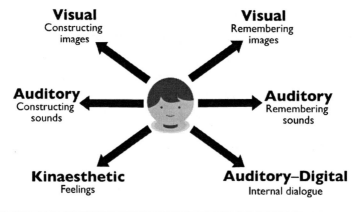

Visual Constructing images

Visual Remembering images

Auditory Constructing sounds

Auditory Remembering sounds

Kinaesthetic Feelings

Auditory–Digital Internal dialogue

Normally organised or reverse organised?

The description above applies if we are right-handed, with a few exceptions. If we write with our left hand, the left-right directions may well be reversed. If our eyes move consistently with the majority of right-handed people, we are said to be "normally organised;" if in the opposite direction, we are "reverse organised." Some people who write with their left hand are reverse organised and some are not. A few right-handed writers are also reverse organised—possibly individuals who are left-side dominant but have learned to write right-handed.

We can observe the predominance of different directions of someone's eye movement and infer relative preferences among the four thinking styles. Frequently looking up suggests visual preference. Moving from side to side suggests auditory. Looking down to their right suggests kinaesthetic. Looking down to their left or gazing over others' heads and appearing detached and dissociated suggests A-D.

Visual people may have difficulty accessing emotions because they tend not to look in the "right" place (down and to the right). Encouraging them to do so can help them articulate their feelings.

From the example file

 An entrepreneur looked down and to his right as he recited facts about his company. As it was unlikely that he was accessing feelings, I suspected he was engaging in internal dialogue to decide what to say and that he was left-handed. Sure enough, when he stood up to write on a board, he held the pen with his left hand.

Steps to take

 When you can observe someone talking, watch the way they move their eyes and see if you can associate that direction with the words they are using at the time and your sense of how they may be thinking. (Bear in mind they may be "reverse organised.")

 Try spelling a word you find difficult from memory. Notice where your eyes go when you do this. Direct your eyes to the opposite side, against the natural process, and notice what that feels like as you spell another word that gives you trouble. Most people report a feeling of discomfort.

 Ask a friend to sit facing you in a relaxed state and notice the direction of the eye movement when you ask these questions:

1. What does your home look like?
2. What would your home look like painted yellow?
3. What was the last thing you said when you left home (or work) today?
4. What would you sound like if you barked like a dog?

5. What are your feelings sitting here now?
6. What are you saying to yourself?

You might find it helpful to have your friend hold this book open with the previous diagram visible to you in such a way that you can see both their face and the illustration at the same time. Once your subject relaxes, you'll see enough to confirm the pattern of movements, accepting you may see only a flicker and sometimes nothing at all. You could try some other questions in the same vein if you don't see the pattern at first. Ask questions that are a little challenging.

We consider eye contact helpful to a relationship, but knowledge of these eye-accessing cues may convince you that we break eye contact for good reason, especially if we have just been asked a searching question. People who are trained to maintain eye contact, such as television journalists and politicians, sometimes seem to move their head around to orient their eyes relative to their head so that they can achieve the accessing effect while still maintaining eye contact.

The origin of our voice, its character, and our breathing

Our voice comes out of our mouth, of course, but its apparent origin varies between individuals. The location indicates something about our preferred thinking style, as does the way we breathe. Here are the patterns:

Visual The voice seems to come from the head or throat area, with a high word rate and a loud, clear, relatively high-pitched quality. Breathing is high up in the chest. With strongly visual people, you may experience difficulty interrupting their speech.

Kinaesthetic The voice appears to come from the abdomen and is low, slow, and soft in character. Breathing is also deep. Kinaesthetic people may take some time to respond to questions as they "feel" for the answer. So if someone is slow to answer questions, it may be they are kinaesthetic, rather than unintelligent.

Auditory Auditory is in between visual and kinaesthetic, with a melodic, rhythmic, variable voice coming from chest-level or ranging from throat to abdomen. Similarly, breathing is anywhere from high in the chest to low in the abdomen.

Auditory-digital The voice is monotonic, clipped, and consistent, and breathing is tight and restricted.

Our body shape, posture, and movement

The shape of our body, our posture, and the way we move offer clues to our preferred representational systems, or in the case of posture and movement, the one we are using at the time.

Visual Body shape is either thin or obese. Posture is straight and upright, with head and shoulders up with tight, jerky movements. The visual person may doodle.

Kinaesthetic Soft, full, and rounded body shape. Posture is curved or bowed, head and shoulders down, with loose and flowing movements. The kinaesthetic person fiddles with things.

Auditory Auditory body shape is in between visual and kinaesthetic, both loose and tight. The head tilted to one side in "telephone" posture is characteristic of auditory.

Auditory-digital Auditory-digital body shape is soft and full with tension in the neck, shoulders, and jaw. Arms folded, head up, erect, with a hand supporting the chin is typical.

Steps to take

 Look out for the non-verbal pointers to thinking-style preferences: location of voice, breathing, body shape, and movement.

Which comes first, the way we think or the way our body is? I believe both go hand-in-hand as part of a consistent pattern of development. If you change the way you breathe, however, you will influence the representational system you use. So if you breathe more deeply, you will think more kinaesthetically and be more in touch with your feelings. If you breathe in a shallow way, you may think more visually. You can experiment with this for yourself.

Which representational system they take us into

Another way of discerning other people's preferences is to notice which representational system they take us into when they are leading the conversation. So if we find ourselves looking at pictures and creating images in our head, that suggests they are visual; if it's all dialogue and sounds, auditory; if we're aware of sensations, feelings, and physical objects, then kinaesthetic; and finally if it's all about thinking and formal-sounding language, the other person is A-D. With a little practice and familiarity with our own experience of the four representational systems, we can sense others' preferences without looking for specific indicators.

Sometimes we find nothing stands out with other people, and we don't know what their preferences are. That can mean that theirs are similar to ours. When it comes to VAK preferences, we tend to notice what's different from us rather than what's the same.

Putting the clues together

So how can we work with all this information? There is no right way, but it may be helpful to set out one approach. We can come by evidence in various different ways, but in real-life situations, we have limited time and attention to devote to working out someone's preferences. If another person seems to have a bit of everything, then that probably means they are relatively balanced in their use of the different representational systems. Remembering that visual is the most common preference, we can start with that.

Visual?
- Are they slim or obese?
- Do they talk quickly and rather a lot?
- Do they draw diagrams or write on flip charts or white boards?
- Do they doodle?
- Do they seem to find the pictures you show them helpful?
- Is their breathing shallow?
- Do they use visual words?
- Do they answer questions quickly?
- Do they look upward often?
- Do they find it difficult to express their feelings?

- Does their voice seem to come from their head and throat area?
- Is their voice relatively high in pitch?
- Do they take you into visual?

If the answer to most or even some of these questions is "yes," then visual is an important part of their make-up. If not, then the next most common is kinaesthetic.

Kinaesthetic?
- Do they have a rounded figure?
- Do they talk slowly and with relatively few words?
- Do physical objects and movement seem important to them?
- Is their breathing deep?
- Do they use kinaesthetic words?
- Is there a delay before they answer questions?
- Do they look down often, especially to their right?
- Do they find it easy to talk about how they feel?
- Does their voice seem to come from low down in their body?
- Is their voice relatively low in pitch?
- Do they take you into kinaesthetic?

If the answer to most of these questions is "yes," that suggests a kinaesthetic preference. If neither visual nor kinaesthetic seem to fit, then they could be in the less common category of auditory.

Auditory?
- Do they seem in between in terms of body appearance, breathing, and voice?
- Are sounds important to them?
- Do they seem to pay attention to the sound of their voice?
- Do they use auditory words?
- Do they play a musical instrument or sing?
- Does their head tilt to one side from time to time?
- Do their eyes move left and right horizontally?
- Do they take you into auditory?

A combination of these attributes would suggest auditory. Finally, a strong auditory-digital preference would be indicated by positive answers to some of the following.

Auditory-digital?

- Do they speak in language that doesn't relate directly to sensory experience?
- Do they use auditory-digital words?
- Do they support their chin with their hand?
- Do they look down and to their left?
- Do they seem a little detached?
- Is their speech clipped?
- Do they seem a little tense?

You can use these questions to figure out your own preferences. Bear in mind that there are no right answers and everybody is a blend of all four representational systems.

Matching representational systems

The most effective way to communicate with people is in their preferred channel or representational system. We are then talking to them the way they talk to themselves and little will be more powerful than that. Show pictures to a visual person or use visual language; describe feelings to a kinaesthetic person or let them handle something or use movement; and concentrate on your speech with an auditory person. If you are still to find out their preference or you are with a group, use all three.

When we seek to match one person, it is usually best to discern their preference and match that. With a group, we can cover the possibilities by starting with kinaesthetic, moving through auditory, and into visual. In this way, we build rapport first with kinaesthetic and then auditory, and take them all into visual.

When people are stuck in a problem, it will often be effective to work on the issue in another channel. For example, visual people will be used to thinking in pictures internally or externally or both, but may have difficulty thinking about and discussing their feelings. They still have emotions and can get upset, but have difficulty talking about it. If they develop their ability to express their feelings, they may well find new routes to solutions. Two individuals whose preferred channels are different may find they can work well by using the third channel that is not the preferred one for either of them—frequently, auditory—and talking more about their issues.

Steps to take

 Make an effort to match the thinking preferences of the people in your relationships. Find the channel of communication that works.

 Use language that is rich in sensory words—that way you will connect with more people.

Representational systems in relationships

As you learn about representational systems, you'll begin to see that you're stuck with individuals that have different VAK and A-D preferences from you. For example, you might realise that you are married to such a person.

In the home and family environment, the issue is one of figuring out preferences over time and finding ways of communicating that are effective. In work situations, we have less time, possibly much less time, to develop a picture of individual people, so we need to make a quick assessment of preferences and then work with that.

VAK preferences are evident in children at a very young age, certainly by age three. If there is more than one child in the family, their choices tend to be complementary, so for example, if the first child is visual, the second is likely to be kinaesthetic or auditory. That means in a family of any size at all, you will have complementary rather than matched VAK preferences, and family communication is likely to benefit from some flexibility in the use of the different channels. For a parent, finding ways of communicating important points visually, by talking, and by touch and feel is likely to help learning.

My wife Catriona has a strong visual preference, and I am mixture of auditory and kinaesthetic as I have mentioned before, so in terms of representational systems, we make a poor match. Fortunately, we seem to be suited in other ways and have survived so far in spite of it all. The VAK mismatch, however, is a serious issue. For example, I remarked recently that I felt differently after completing a task, and I meant a significant change. Catriona's neutral response indicated that my statement didn't connect with her. If I had said that I saw myself differently, then she would have understood what I meant.

The visual appearance of things matters more to Catriona than it does to me. I would tend to emphasise the physical feel of things and their function. The result is we have different priorities about what should be improved in and around our house, and sometimes we argue about that, although the eventual benefit is a balanced overall approach to running the home. Because our VAK preferences are largely unconscious, we're usually not aware of the conflicted criteria right up until the point of decision— at which time, suddenly there is an unforeseen clash. We're not alone in having this kind of challenge.

We have found over the years that communicating in the kinaesthetic channel—and that means hugs really—is the reliable way for us to get over an argument, especially when words and pictures don't do the job. With the physical contact, less needs to be articulated consciously and we can reassure each other that we don't mean to argue, even though we might still be at odds over the specific issue.

When you tune in

Developing your awareness of your own preferred representational systems will open your eyes to how much your unconscious choices in this area colour your life and your relationships, and how you might make adjustments to adapt to the people around you.

Use of the different channels conveys information at different rates. Auditory is the slowest because it's at the one-dimensional pace of word-by-word, but it's also versatile. Visual is two-dimensional and faster—"A picture is worth a thousand words." Kinaesthetic is fastest of all because it encompasses everything and is three-dimensional. Touch of some kind communicates a great deal very quickly. However, as Richard Bandler and John Grinder said: "No special one of the representational systems available is better than the others, although some may be more efficient for certain tasks."

Many of us use a blend of the channels, while others live at the extremes of visual, kinaesthetic, and auditory preference and thus experience a very different life.

Step 4: Wavelength

In summary

- We have several representational systems and varying preferences about how much we use each one:
  - Visual (images)
  - Auditory (sound)
  - Kinaesthetic (feelings and sensations)
  - Auditory-digital (internal dialogue)

- VAK preferences show themselves in various ways:
  - Words used
  - Eye movements
  - Sound of the voice
  - Breathing
  - Body shape and movement
  - Posture

- Aim to match other people's preferences and, by doing so, talk to them the way they talk to themselves.

- Our habitual choice of visual, auditory, kinaesthetic, and auditory-digital thinking affects our lives and our relationships much more than we probably realise.

Relating to you

- Who could you do a better job of tuning in to?

- What's the biggest learning you have taken from this chapter?

Step 5:
Filters

Understanding personality

Before *You may:*	After *You will:*
✘ Be unaware that you automatically filter the information you receive	✔ Understand filters and the effect they have on personality
✘ Assume that we all filter things the same way	✔ Know what the more significant filters are and how to work with them
✘ Be manipulated by people who have the skills to work with filtering patterns	✔ Be able to discern and match others' filters
✘ Be blind to the unconscious choices you make about what to focus on	✔ Appreciate the impact that unconscious filtering patterns have on your life and your relationships
✘ Mismatch other people without realising	✔ Have the awareness to adjust your filtering patterns to suit the results you want
	✔ Know how to make a proposal to someone in a way they will accept

Step 5: Filters

Where we place our attention determines much of what happens in our lives and our relationships, and yet most of our choices about what to focus on are made unconsciously and automatically. Each of us has a range of filtering processes at a deep and unconscious level, and these make us much more different from each other than we probably realise. This is the stuff of personality. Various models are available to make sense of this picture, all based on the work of Carl Jung. The best-known example is the Myers-Briggs Type Indicator® (MBTI®)[1]. In NLP, the equivalent topic is "metaprogrammes," and three of the four MBTI types map to NLP metaprogrammes. The relationship with the fourth is a little more complex.

Filtering in, filtering out

The information we take in depends on what we are paying attention to, and this in turn depends on our values and beliefs, sense of identity, past experiences, and filtering patterns. The vast majority of the processing our brains apply to the information we receive from our senses goes on unconsciously. In fact, our conscious mind has the ability to pay attention to only a small number of things concurrently: seven plus or minus two, according to research by George Miller published in 1956. Our conscious mind is like a radio tuning in to a small number of signals out of many channels of communication. One consequence of this is that most of the information processing going on in a relationship is happening unconsciously.

We filter the information we receive from our senses. If we didn't, we would be overwhelmed with data. The filters we apply determine which sensory information we pay attention to, and therefore our perceptions, thinking patterns, emotional state, and ultimately, our actions and responses. There's a little more to it than that, however, because we tend to act (as well as sense) in accordance with our filtering patterns. For example, if we filter for details, we act in the details as well.

Most filtering patterns involve a spectrum between extremes, such as between "big picture" and "details," and we prefer different points on these spectra, depending on our experiences and the context. As Tad

1. Myers-Briggs Type Indicator and MBTI are registered trademarks of the Myers-Briggs Type Indicator Trust.

James and Wyatt Woodsmall said: "The use of one pattern is not right and another wrong. Some patterns are more useful in certain contexts than others." All have consequences. In the context of relationships, as opposed to survival as a hunter-gatherer, for example, some filtering patterns may lead to unhelpful results. Gaining conscious awareness of the filters that we apply opens up the possibility of increasing the range of the filtering patterns we use and consequently, the flexibility of our responses to particular situations and of course, relationships. Observing filtering patterns in others can also offer an increased awareness and understanding of what is going on.

The Myers-Briggs model is mainly concerned with eliciting individuals' filtering patterns and accepting them as they are. This "profiling" is helpful, but may cause people to feel that they can't do anything about their own filtering patterns. NLP, in contrast, is concerned with developing flexibility and becoming mindful of what is going on in the moment. If a filtering pattern has consequences we don't like, we might choose to alter it. One of the ways that people become adaptable is by being able to vary the filtering patterns they run, for example, in the details one minute and then up in the big picture the next—sometimes referred to as "chunking up." Our filtering patterns do change through time, and we tend to become more flexible as we get older.

We can use questionnaires to elicit filtering patterns, which is the basis of the MBTI "Instrument," but in day-to-day life, we need a spontaneous approach. With a little practice, we can discern filtering patterns by observing other people and asking carefully crafted questions as the opportunity arises. In this chapter, we'll look at examples that can be tailored to your particular context. The best approach is to understand the principles and then adapt them to your circumstances. With a little ingenuity, you will be able to ask appropriate questions in the normal course of conversation.

With all of the filtering patterns, being mindful of our own programming and alive to that of the other person takes us at least halfway to understanding what the consequences are likely to be and how we might accommodate them. We also become aware of how our own filtering is likely to affect the information we receive and the information we may miss. As Tad James and Wyatt Woodsmall said, the purpose of looking at filtering patterns is not "to be able to put people in little boxes." Instead, "use them to make people's lives, including your own, better."

Specific filtering patterns

We'll start with one of the filtering patterns that is likely to be familiar to you already.

Small chunk (details)—Big chunk (concepts)

We all probably know someone who is a "detail person" but seems unable to "see the big picture" or conversely, someone who is "broad-brush" but who fails to "pay attention to detail." Where we sit on this spectrum from details to concepts, or "small chunk" to "big chunk," can be an area of mismatch in a relationship. This mismatch may be a strength because the people are complementary, but it can lead to communication difficulties.

To help us understand what is happening, we can find out someone's preference with a question like:

> *If we were working on something together, would you want to know the big picture first or the details first?*

Having discovered their preference, to find out whether the other extreme matters at all, we could ask about the opposite:

> *Would you really need to know the details?* or
> *Would you really need to know the big picture?*

The answer will indicate whether their preference is details or big picture only, or whether they like to start with one and then progress to the other.

Steps to take

- If you're inclined to focus on the details, reflect on what might change if you paid more attention to the context and overall direction of what you are doing. Are you focused on the right details? At the other extreme, if you disregard the details, what issues might you be overlooking?

- Once you have figured out someone's preference, match them by presenting details or concepts as appropriate and then move toward the other end of the spectrum as required.

Self—Others

Another important filtering distinction is whether we sort for ourselves or for others. Do we attend to others or do we attend to ourselves? This was the subject matter of "Step 1: Attention to others," in which we developed our flexibility to change this filtering pattern, in particular to filter for others when that is going to help our relationships.

As Tad James and Wyatt Woodsmall put it: "The person who filters by others is willing to enter other people's models of the world. The best managers, salespeople, therapists, and communicators filter by others."

We can determine whether other people are filtering for themselves or for others just by observing them.

Away from—Toward

We may talk articulately and at length about what we don't want or don't like, filtering for movement away from a problem, or we may focus on moving toward something we do want or like. We can discern someone's pattern either by observing what they say or asking them a question, such as:

What do you want in a _____? or
What's important to you about _____?

Here, we fill in the blank with a topic that seems important to the other person. The extent to which the answer consists of things that are not wanted versus things that are wanted will indicate whether they filter for:

- Toward
- Toward with a little away
- Both toward and away equally
- Away with a little toward
- Away

Encouraging each type to look at things the other way can often be highly effective in problem situations.

From the example file

 When children play with sand in an indoor sandbox, in a nursery for example, they tend to spill some of it. Instead of saying, "Don't get the sand on the floor," it's much better to say to them, "Keep the sand in the box." It even feels different saying it. Our focus is in a different place. The energy feels channeled. Similarly, we're more likely to get the outcome we want if we say to children, "Stay in bed," rather than "Don't get up."

Sameness—Difference (Matcher—Mismatcher)

When we come across new things, including people and what they say, we compare them with what we already know (our model of the world). Some individuals see what's different and others notice what's the same, both then commenting on their observations. The person who speaks about what's different—the mismatcher—can tax the rapport in the relationship, whereas the person who highlights sameness is likely to build rapport. As Tad James and Wyatt Woodsmall said, "Both matching and mismatching are important in business," with accountants, lawyers, and engineers implicitly trained to be mismatchers, and salespeople to be matchers.

A suitable question to elicit this pattern is something like the following, asked in the context in which you want to know their filtering pattern—home or work, for example:

How does what you are doing this year compare with what you were doing last year?

The answer will indicate whether they filter for:

- Sameness
- Sameness with some difference
- Sameness and difference equally
- Difference with some sameness
- Difference

Sue Knight points out that: "You can easily notice someone who prefers to mismatch—they stand out from a group as the one whose behaviour is different to the rest."

Steps to take

 Are you a mismatcher—always looking for what's different and what's not right about what you see or hear? Be aware that this behaviour can be tiring for other people and consider looking instead for what's the same and what's right.

 If you are dealing with a mismatcher, you may find that it helps to say, "I know you won't like this, but..." or something similar. The mismatcher is then likely to counter your presumption that they won't like your point rather than the point itself.

I was a mismatcher through most of my twenties and thirties. I used to think it was vital to point out what was wrong with things so that errors could be corrected and success ensured—probably the consequence of an in-depth education and training as an engineer, where the emphasis is on solving problems. Unfortunately, this behaviour wasn't always appreciated. Others found that what they saw as "nitpicking" hindered their efforts to make progress toward the goal. Mismatching damages rapport, that's the problem. As Sue Knight said, "This kind of behaviour is characteristic of someone who may have difficulty in relationships, who may not be easy to converse with, and who seems to put obstacles in the path of any connectedness to anyone else." (That was me, for sure. I hope I'm not quite so annoying now.)

I changed my filter (and so my behaviour) when my boss at the time pointed it out. I found it easy to change once I realised what I was doing. Toning down mismatching behaviour and replacing it with matching is an easy thing to do, and the benefit is well worth the effort involved. The change has smoothed my relationships a great deal.

Internally referenced—Externally referenced (Introvert—Extrovert)

People who are strongly internally referenced make up their own mind about things and are rarely swayed by others' opinions. Conversely, externally referenced people are influenced by what other people say.

We can elicit this filtering pattern by asking questions such as:

How do you know when you're doing a good job? or
How would you know when you've found the right _____?

Answers such as "I just know" indicate internal reference, whereas "because my boss tells me" indicates external reference.

The answer will indicate whether their frame of reference is:

* Internal
* Internal with external check
* Balanced
* External with internal check
* External

External with an internal check means that they seek the opinion of a number of others and then check that they are happy with the conclusion. Internal with external check means that they come to a decision within themselves and then check that others agree with it.

The internal/external referencing filtering pattern is equivalent to the Introvert—Extrovert distinction in the Myers Briggs model. (This differs from using the word "extrovert" to describe someone who is "the life of the party.")

Internally referenced people can sometimes be indifferent to what other people want; however, others will know where they stand with them. Individuals who are externally referenced may take silence as approval withheld and stay in an insecure state as a result. They may also neglect their own interest.

Steps to take

 Ponder your own internal/external referencing. How much do you depend on other people to form your opinions and how much do you make up your own mind? What benefits might flow from adjusting your habits and being a little more flexible in this area?

Possibility—Necessity (Perceiver—Judger)

People who filter for possibility look for the opportunity in a situation, whereas those who filter for necessity look for guidelines and rules. Necessity filterers (also known as "judgers" in the MBTI model) do well with clear procedures and guidelines, but may be less creative and may have difficulty in unstructured situations. Judgers tend to have a strong adherence to time schedules and will live a more orderly, detailed, planned existence. Possibility filterers ("perceivers") are likely to be innovative and will be effective in fluid, ambiguous situations, but may be poor at adhering to procedures and systems, including ones they create themselves, and may be reluctant to make decisions that close down their options.

We can discern something about this filter in a conversation with another person by making a very open request of them, such as asking them to say a bit about themselves. Possibility filterers will launch into whatever it suits them to talk about, whereas necessity filterers will ask for some guidance on the desired focus of the subject matter.

You can also elicit this metaprogramme by asking:

What are your reasons for choosing to do what you're doing?

The answer will indicate whether they are filtering for possibility (if they talk about opportunities) or necessity (if they talk about rules), or perhaps a bit of both.

Another approach is:

> *If we were working on a project together, would you like to have a definite plan that we stick to, or would you like to be able to make changes as we go along?*

A desire for flexibility indicates a "perceiver" pattern. A preference for certainty suggests a "judger."

Steps to take

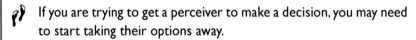 If you are trying to get a perceiver to make a decision, you may need to start taking their options away.

If you are a perceiver yourself, you may be uncomfortable pushing someone else to make a decision because you dislike cutting down your own options. Be aware of the consequences of your pattern.

Convincer pattern

Individuals vary in the amount that they need to experience something before they are convinced, ranging from automatically convinced, through needing several repetitions or a length of time, to needing consistent experience of the evidence to remain convinced. Needing to see or hear things about three times is rather common—the "three-times convincer," as is just needing one experience—the "one-time convincer" pattern.

You can elicit convincer pattern by asking a question such as:

> *How often does someone have to demonstrate competence to you before you're convinced?*

The answer will indicate whether their convincer pattern is:

- Automatic
- Number of times
- Period of time
- Consistent

Listening style and speaking style

We can be either a literal listener who takes what's said at face value or an inferential listener who interprets a comment and decides what to do about it. Similarly, we can be literal or inferential in our speaking style. We can observe these traits in others and ourselves.

We can elicit listening style by observing or asking a question such as:

If someone you knew quite well said to you, "I'm hungry," would you find the comment interesting but probably do nothing about it, or would you feel that you needed to do something about it?

If they just found the comment interesting, that would be literal listening, whereas taking action would imply inferential listening. We can elicit speaking style by observing or asking a question such as:

If you felt that someone you knew quite well was not performing as well as they should, would you tell them directly or would you hint, imply, or give them clues about the problem?

Dissociated—Associated (Thinker—Feeler)

This filtering pattern is related to the Myers-Briggs "Thinking—Feeling" distinction. When someone is emotionally engaged in a situation, they are said to be "associated"—they are living the experience. People who are "dissociated" ("thinkers") are hanging back from emotional engagement and can seem cool and aloof. They are likely to use A-D language in their speech, among other things.

In NLP, the word "uptime" is used to refer to a state in which our sensory awareness is fully applied to our external environment and we are fully "present." As Robert Dilts wrote: "Uptime, and the increased amount of sensory experience that comes from uptime, helps us to more fully perceive and enjoy life and the many possibilities for learning that surround us."

Past—Present—Future

Some people are inclined to "live in the past" and cherish traditions, whereas others look forward to the future. Some are focused on the present, rather to the exclusion of both the past and the future.

Long term—Short term

Filtering for the short term means looking at things that will be important in the near or very near future, whereas filtering for the long term means looking at things that will be important at a much greater distance of time, for example, over years or a lifetime. We can see different "long-term—short-term" filtering preferences in the behaviour of investment markets—between one country and another, for instance.

Task—Relationship

Task-oriented people focus on getting things done, sometimes at the expense of their relationships with other people. Relationship-oriented people, on the other hand, can sometimes fail to achieve an objective because of their focus on preserving relationships.

Being mindful of filters

We could work our way through all the different filtering patterns, but it would be too much, as about sixty have been described. We've covered the more significant ones—this is quite enough to work with and open your eyes to how important these automatic processes are and how you might benefit from being mindful of them. Just being aware that we make different choices is a good start. Because of the deep-seated nature of our filters, the changes we make to our patterns have profound effects.

Tad James and Wyatt Woodsmall observed that metaprogrammes are "culturally independent, although the percentages of people in a certain category may differ from culture to culture."

Each filtering pattern or metaprogramme is a study in itself, and books have been written solely on the subject of filtering patterns. One well-known one is Shelle Rose Charvet's *Words That Change Minds*. A section of Tad James and Wyatt Woodsmall's book *Timeline Therapy and the Basis of Personality* is also devoted to this subject.

The fourth and final Myers-Briggs distinction ("Intuitor—Sensor") relates to a combination of metaprogrammes and also has a relationship with representational systems (see "Step 4: Wavelength"). An intuitor may have a stronger preference for A-D thinking than a sensor. A sensor is more interested in facts, and an intuitor is more interested in ideas.

Put all these filtering patterns together with the VAK representational systems we covered in "Step 4: Wavelength," and we end up with many ways in which individual preferences and personality traits arise. We are a diverse bunch. Perhaps that's the most important learning. Much of what happens in our relationships arises because we are different and what's more, we mostly don't realise just how different we are. Our filtering is largely unconscious. To illustrate: When we buy a new car, we're blind to examples of the model until we take an interest in it. We just don't see them out there. All our filtering patterns affect us in the same way. We're just as blind to things in our relationships we happen not to be filtering for—stuff is whizzing past and we just don't notice.

Steps to take

🐾 In your relationships, be open to the possibility that differences of filtering patterns are making their presence felt all the time. If you're having problems, it's likely that you're mismatched somewhere. What do you notice is different about the other person against some of the headings we have covered? Once you have identified a problem area, work out ways to change what you do. Often that will be enough to unblock the situation. For example, as I said before, if people keep talking about what they don't want, ask them what they do want. They can talk all day about what they don't want, but it doesn't give you anything to work with because you can't deliver an absence of something.

🐾 With a little practice, you can gather information about filtering patterns in casual conversation just by noticing what people say and asking appropriate questions as the opportunities arise. You'll then be able to tailor what you say to their preferences.

🐾 As an exercise with a friend, identify some of their filtering patterns using the questions we have covered and then prepare and make a proposal to them (for example, to join you on a trip somewhere) in a way that is suited to their preferences. See if they are persuaded. Review and swap roles.

In this exercise, when it's done well, we don't notice when our preferences are played back to us. We're not conscious of the filtering we're doing. My experience is sitting, waiting to notice the first filtering pattern being played back to me, but not noticing any at all before the other person has finished their "pitch." That illustrates how unconscious we are of these patterns. It's only if the other gets it a bit wrong that we notice. If what's said is a good match, we're sold.

Step 5: Filters

In summary

We unconsciously filter the information we receive and have different preferences about what we filter for.

The more significant filtering patterns are:

- Small chunk—Big chunk
- Self—Others
- Away from—Toward
- Sameness—Difference
- Internally referenced—Externally referenced
- Possibility—Necessity
- Convincer pattern
- Inferential—Literal listener/speaker
- Dissociated—Associated
- Past—Present—Future
- Long term—Short term
- Task—Relationship

The effects of these preferences can be pervasive but out of our awareness.

We can spot or elicit others' filtering preferences and notice our own.

We can improve our relationships by aligning what we say and do with other people's filtering preferences.

Relating to you

Which of your relationships would benefit from some different filtering?

Which filter has the greatest impact on your life?

Step 6: Connection

Regarding rapport as a resource

Before	After
You may:	*You will:*
✘ Rely on finding subjects in common to connect with people	✔ Be aware of whether or not you are in rapport with people
✘ Regard body language as something to interpret and no more	✔ Use non-verbal channels of communication
✘ Be unaware of whether or not you are in rapport with someone	✔ Be able to connect with people quickly, easily, and reliably
✘ Break rapport without realising or intending to	✔ Be able to assess whether the time is right to make a challenging request, such as ask for the sale
✘ Struggle to connect with people	✔ Think of connection as something to nurture
✘ Block connection by not being yourself	✔ Be able to sense what is going on for people and what their feelings are
	✔ Know how to connect at a deeper and stronger level if you choose

Step 6: Connection

A feeling of connection with other people is one of life's greatest pleasures, wherever it arises, and it's also one our greatest resources. We can strengthen our capacity to connect with people in several ways: by improving our ability to build rapport and by finding ways to touch people emotionally. Both deepen our relationships and make them rich and enduring.

Investing in rapport with other people ensures that a connection is there when we need it. When we seek to achieve something in a relationship, if we don't have enough rapport, we won't get the result we want. Without rapport with other people, we will not succeed with them—we won't make the sale, get the date, or whatever. With rapport, on the other hand, most things are easy. So we can think of rapport as a resource to be nurtured, protected, and when necessary, drawn on.

To begin a relationship, we need to connect with the other person. We can achieve that in two ways: with the subject matter we talk about and with non-verbal, rapport-building behaviour—a natural process normally outside our conscious awareness. Whether we are meeting strangers, catching up with someone we know, or interacting with people we deal with fleetingly in everyday life, we can accelerate the development of rapport and make the results more certain.

Is deliberate rapport-building manipulative?

With non-verbal rapport skills, we are making conscious something that happens unconsciously anyway. We already do various things on purpose to increase rapport. For example, we dress in a manner to fit in, but we don't see that as manipulative. We may as well take the extra step and control our non-verbal communication too.

Non-verbal communication

The notion of "body language" has become well known, and no doubt we can gather some meaning from posture and gestures if we treat our inferences with caution. A "this means that" approach is too crude, though. Mastery in relationship skills involves something related but more subtle, and the benefits of working in the non-verbal dimensions are not so widely understood. Body language is often regarded as something to observe, but we can actively communicate in the non-verbal channels too.

We are conditioned culturally to regard the words people say as the true meaning of what they are communicating, but if there are contradictory signals in posture, gesture, and tone of voice, these non-verbal elements are much more likely to reflect the reality of what people think and feel than the words they say.

The first to study the distribution of meaning between verbal and non-verbal channels was Albert Mehrabian in 1972. He found that up to 93 percent of the meaning of what we communicate resides not in our words, but in the non-verbal information we provide while delivering our words—i.e., how we say them (38 percent) and how we seem when we say them (55 percent).

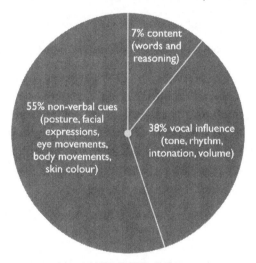

So how our communication is received depends on how we look, how we sound, and what we say, in descending order of importance, with our actual words at the bottom of the list. We can draw a number of conclusions from this:

- If we invest all our energy in the words we say, we are using only seven percent of the potential communication channel available to us.

- We communicate to others continuously, even when sitting still and silently.

- More than half of the communication with another person is going on irrespective of who is speaking at the time and can flow in both directions simultaneously.

- We could benefit from paying more attention to our non-verbal communication, whether we are listening or speaking.

- We can use non-verbal communication to build rapport.

Rapport

Rapport is easier to experience than define or describe, partly because people sense it in different ways. If we are in rapport with someone, we might describe them as "coming from the same place," "seeing things the same way," "speaking the same language," or being "on the same wavelength." Rapport involves a sense of being at ease and communicating freely (or perhaps an absence of unease).

My dictionary defines rapport as:

relation: connection: sympathy: emotional bond: spiritualistic touch

The most useful of these for our purposes is "emotional bond," especially if we mean anything that happens beyond a fleeting, emotionless interaction. An example of an interaction without rapport is handing a ticket to a member of staff in a railway station. We have no emotional engagement. As soon as there is any eye contact, conversation, or perhaps physical assistance, however, we have the possibility of an emotional response and rapport beginning.

Roget's Thesaurus offers some related words that allude to other aspects of rapport:

relation, relatedness, connectedness, respect, regard, concern, interest, involvement, attraction, affinity, interdependence, harmony, unison, understanding, reciprocity

We are either in rapport with someone or we aren't, with little gray zone in between, and we can move from one state to the other rather quickly. Rapport is two-way. We can't be in rapport unless the other person is too.

Steps to take

 When you interact with another person with whom your relationship is easy, relaxed, and enjoyable, notice your feelings and emotional state. Contrast that with another situation where you have no

---

relationship, perhaps because you have only just met. In the first case you are in rapport, in the second, not—at least at first. Notice how you tell whether you are in rapport and what happens when you do connect for the first time. Becoming consciously aware of the signals is a useful skill to develop.

Rapport happens (or not) whether the relationship is mainly face-to-face, on the phone, by email, or by letter. The way you experience rapport may be different in each case.

Rapport develops between people who sense they are like each other in some way. We can list some of the many possible dimensions in a rough order, from ones we are consciously aware of down to others we are usually quite unaware of:

- The day's events: weather, travel, news
- Shared experiences and interests: books, films, places
- Mutual acquaintances
- Work role
- Family context
- Physical appearance and dress
- Use of language
- Posture
- Breathing
- Voice
- Values
- VAK thinking preferences
- Filtering patterns

We can see from the length of the list that we are unlikely ever to align with someone on every heading, but the number of variables also means that similarity on some points can be more significant than mismatch or even conflict on others. That means we can be in rapport even if we have differences.

The items down as far as physical appearance, dress, and use of language are familiar enough aspects of finding common ground with other people and are not something we'll say much more about here, apart from a reminder about the benefits we covered in "Step 1: Attention to Others." Let other people talk about their subjects.

We looked in detail at VAK preferences in "Step 4: Wavelength" and at filtering patterns in "Step 5: Filters." We will cover values in the next chapter. All of these have an important part to play in connecting with other people. In Step 6, we cover the non-verbal aspects of building rapport.

In the normal course of a relationship, starting from the first meeting, we build rapport consciously through the discovery of things in common and unconsciously through noticing similarities. At the conscious level, we employ a variety of conversational conventions, starting by talking about the weather or our journey, for example, before moving on to weightier matters. With a little practice, we can also attune to the automatic building and nurturing of non-verbal rapport and give the natural process a helping hand.

Listening with care and skill is often still a minority occupation in organisations. People who do take the trouble to build rapport and to listen tend to have influence and be treated with respect.

Building rapport in the non-verbal dimension

We can focus on three main aspects to promote non-verbal rapport:

- Our posture and movement
- Our breathing
- Our voice

Matching our level of energy is also important. One of the presuppositions we covered in "Step 2: Attitude" is at work here:

Mind and body are part of the same system.
Change one and you affect the other.

We use this principle by working with our bodies to influence the mind—either our own or the other person's.

Our posture and movement

We can build rapport by moving ourselves to reflect the way another person positions the various parts of their body, whether they are still or moving. By doing this, we take control of our own body language or "physiology" in NLP jargon. We can match or mirror many different aspects:

- General posture (i.e., leaning forward or back and/or to the side)
- Position of the shoulders
- Tilt of the head
- Facial expression
- Leg, foot, arm, hand, and finger positions
- Gestures
- Movements and changes in position

Matching and mirroring is a dynamic process, like being in a dance together. When you are speaking, use the same gestures as the other person does when they are speaking. Detail is important, so pay attention to the position and movement of fingers and the elements of facial expressions.

Building rapport like this can seem like mimicry, but in fact, the unease stems from making an unconscious process conscious. As Tad James and David Shephard put it, "In general, people aren't consciously aware of what they are doing with their own physiology, let alone what someone else is doing with theirs."

Match or mirror?

We can either match or mirror. If the other person leans to their left and we lean to our left, we are matching. To mirror, we lean to our right when they lean to their left. Matching and mirroring both work, but mirroring is easier. Here, we'll use both words interchangeably.

Due to gender differences, it's sometimes inappropriate to match or mirror exactly, particularly leg positions. If that's an issue, choose other ways of reflecting body language. Avoid postures that are inappropriate or difficult for the other sex to match or mirror; otherwise, you inhibit the natural process, and the other person may sense a barrier in the relationship without being aware of the reason why.

Steps to take

 With a friend, try discussing a subject on which you agree, and as you do so, mismatch posture and movement. Then try discussing a subject on which you disagree. This time, try matching. Most people find that mismatching tends to inhibit the conversation even when they agree, while matching makes it hard to keep a disagreement going. In the second case, participants report that they end up liking each other anyway. (In this exercise, you could choose not to tell your friend what you are up to and see what happens.)

 Match or mirror people you meet in your daily life and notice what difference it makes, particularly when meeting someone for the first time.

Our breathing

Matching someone else's breathing creates a strong rapport-building effect, by aligning with a vital function of their body. One way of doing this is to watch the movements of their chest, face, or clothing and breathe in time with that. Milton Erickson used this technique to great effect in his work as a hypnotherapist. At another level, humour and jokes are effective for building rapport partly because they cause us to breathe in time with each other as we laugh.

Our voice

The way we use our voice makes an important contribution to whether we achieve rapport with someone or not, as it carries around 38 percent of the meaning of our communication. Again, there are many different elements:

- Pitch (high or low, monotone or melodic)
- Tempo (fast or slow)
- Quality (smooth, rough, or clear)
- Volume (loud or quiet)
- Content chunks (amount said between pauses)
- Rhythm
- Origins (where the voice comes from—high up in the head, low down in the abdomen, or somewhere in between)
- Accents

Rather than pay attention to each of these aspects individually, we may find it easier just to think of making our voice sound like the other person's. With accents, it is best to adjust ours slightly to suit rather than aim for imitation.

We have another gender issue to note here: we don't want to attempt to match pitch exactly, but for example, if a woman speaks in a relatively high-pitched voice (for a woman), then a man speaking to her will build rapport more easily by speaking in a relatively high-pitched voice for a man.

Steps to take

 With two friends, practise matching voices. "Alex" and "Sam" are joined by "Jo" this time. Alex and Sam sit back-to-back. Alex says something like, "Hello, my name is Alex" (or whatever his real name is). Sam repeats what Alex has said, attempting to match Alex's voice. If Alex feels that Sam has been successful and experiences a feeling of rapport, he says so; otherwise, Alex says his sentence again and Sam has another go, with Jo suggesting what changes Sam should make to her voice. (Jo hears both voices externally to her body and so is better placed to notice similarities and differences.) Continue until Sam achieves a match, then rotate roles. Develop this further by making Sam's task to respond to Alex in conversation, while matching his voice.

The ability to build rapport with voice is, of course, particularly important on the telephone.

How much matching and mirroring do we need to do?

Doing every single possible thing in matching or mirroring someone else may not be necessary. Making ourselves seem like the other person in the non-verbal domain will be enough to make a significant difference to how quickly we establish rapport and are accepted by them.

We can choose which of the many aspects to match or mirror. The principle is to adapt ourselves enough to suit the other person rather than mimic them in every way. To gain their trust and help them with a challenging personal problem, we might match and mirror very thoroughly, but everyday situations may require less diligence. As a minimum, avoid mismatching the other person. You may be surprised how much effect even some reflection of the other person's posture and movement can have.

Pacing and leading

We go through two stages with rapport: pacing and leading. Pacing comes first and involves reflecting the other person. Leading follows when rapport has been established and the other person unconsciously matches us, by for example, crossing their legs when we cross our legs or by copying a hand gesture. In the pacing stage, we let the other person lead us. They unconsciously accept that we are similar and sense that we are paying attention to them.

We can test whether we are in rapport with someone by trying to lead them by leaning forward, for example, or changing the position of our arms. If they follow, we are in rapport. If not, we have more pacing to do. We can use this to test whether the time is right to introduce a challenging subject of conversation, such as asking for commitment, but without referring to the new topic at all.

The question arises of what to do with people who appear to have "closed" body language such as folded arms. NLP thinking is that the folded arms may not necessarily indicate a "closed" state, and the best approach is to mirror, build rapport, and eventually lead the person to an open posture.

Steps to take

- Experiencing resistance in people is a sign of lack of rapport. If, in putting an idea, proposal, or request to others, you sense you are meeting resistance, focus on building more rapport rather than trying to strengthen your argument.

- You may notice others unconsciously matching you. You change position and they change position. That means you are leading in the rapport process and, for the time being, in the relationship as well.

- In groups that are in rapport, you may notice a "rapport leader"— one the others all follow. In a business context, it could be the boss, but maybe not. To build rapport with the group, build rapport with the rapport leader. It's likely that the rapport leader is the person who makes the decisions, even if he or she isn't the boss.

Reading emotions and "sensory acuity"

Precisely matching another person's posture and movement builds rapport and also gives us insight into their emotions because we tend to experience the same state that they are in, particularly if we pay attention to the fine details.

Steps to take

🦶 When you are walking in a public place and people are walking in front of you, walk the way one of them walks, with their posture and gait, for ten paces or so. (Be careful to be discreet and respectful in doing this.) Notice how your emotional state changes. What insights do you gain into what is going on for the other person? You might be shocked at some of the feelings you experience and at their intensity.

🦶 Try accessing emotional states with two friends—"Alex," "Sam," and "Jo" again.

1. Place two chairs back-to-back.

2. Alex sits in one chair and Sam in the other so that they cannot see each other.

3. Alex thinks of a situation driving a strong emotion. Alex relives the experience, takes on the emotional state, and lets his body assume the posture that goes with it.

4. Jo now asks Sam to recreate the same physical posture, giving instructions to Sam to adjust the position of her body, piece by piece, progressively refining the detail until the match with Alex is as accurate as possible. Detail is important, especially facial expression and the position of the hands and fingers.

5. Once Jo is finished, Sam describes the emotional state she now experiences and the sense she has of what Alex's situation is.

6. Compare and review insights.

7. Repeat the process, rotating the roles.

You could also do this exercise standing up, provided that Alex and Sam cannot see each other.

Typically, participants are amazed at the detail they pick up about the other person, demonstrating how much can be "read" from a person's posture.

When you realise you can decipher someone's "body language" in detail by "trying on" their posture, working with the meaning of individual gestures seems a crude approach in comparison. Also, we have no need to memorise what specific gestures signify when we can access the whole state.

It's possible to do a version of the previous exercise with just two people sitting face-to-face. One takes on a state and the other matches. It can seem a bizarre thing to do, but the learning is the same. You'll have a laugh anyway.

The experience of these exercises shows we can indeed infer something about other people's states from their body language, but the process is a little more subtle than "this gesture means that." After these exercises, you will find that you are much more able to "read" another person's state and discover what is going on for them—the art of "sensory acuity"—picking up on the signals available. In a way, it's just a matter of gaining confidence that the inklings you have probably are telling you what you think they might be telling you.

Sensory acuity is a core NLP skill and a useful one to develop. We come to realise we can read a great deal, and that others can read us in the same way. We may decide speaking honestly and openly is a good idea, because if we don't, we can be found out very easily.

As you practise building rapport with people and paying attention to their body language, you become much more aware of what is happening around you. That is sensory acuity. From this flows the art of timing, as you become much more aware of the right moment to speak or act.

Keeping rapport once you've got it

One of the main threats to rapport is using the wrong words, and one serial offender is "but." To the listener or reader, the use of "but" may, in essence, "delete" everything that went before it, whether in written or spoken communication. With a bit of thought, we can avoid this problem.

Try replacing "but" with "and" or "and so." This may change the meaning to something that is resourceful and will protect rapport. Instead of "I agree with you, but I think you should also consider this point," use "I agree with you, and I think you should also consider this point." Another possibility is to swap the order of the statements, so instead of "I will try to do it, but it will be difficult," use "It will be difficult, but I will try to do it."

Another approach is to use "even though" instead of "but." For example, instead of "I found a solution to my problem, but it could come back again later," it's better to say, "I found a solution to my problem, even though it could come again later."

Connecting at a deeper level

To connect with people deeply, we need to speak from the heart rather than the head. The more we hide behind layers of protection, the more difficulty others will have relating to us. If we are honest and open, we will find it easier to connect with other people. If they experience us as real, they will be open to us.

Being honest and open might seem to make us vulnerable, but paradoxically, we can find safety in vulnerability because an open disposition is respected, whereas a closed one is attacked. When we pretend we are something we are not, others are distrustful of us, criticise our actions, and keep their distance.

From the example file

 The head of an institution is inclined to talk at people rather than with them and creates little sense of connection. For example, he will deliver a talk to a group of visitors from behind a lectern and by reading a script. The audience is glad when it's over. He could do with learning from his chairman, who is a model of pacing other people and attending to them.

I aim to connect with the people I work with. Perhaps that's a luxury, but I find working with someone without a connection an empty experience that isn't sustainable for long. On getting to know people, I am looking for an opportunity to establish some emotional bond. I find that the quickest way to get to an outcome.

When I was about ten, after an incident in which I fell out with a neighbouring child, my grandmother said, "David, you need all the friends you can get." I didn't really understand at the time, but 35 years later, I know she was right. That was probably the most important thing she ever said to me.

Although I have no brothers or sisters, I had the good fortune to grow up close to a neighbouring family. Now, decades later, I don't see the family members all that often, but when I do, the intervening time falls away and we pick up where we left off. That's connection.

Somebody once said to me that if we split up with a partner, the relationship doesn't come to an end, it just continues in a different form, even if we aren't in touch with the other person any more. I have found that a comforting thought. Love can still flow. Similarly, after people close to us pass away, we can still be connected to them.

Steps to take

- Take away the layers. Be yourself.

- Rapport is like fuel in the tank, so look after it like the precious commodity it is.

- Look out for opportunities to deepen rapport with people, so you will have more to draw on when you need it.

- Remember who your friends (and allies) are and be careful not to damage your connection with them. You may need their support.

The more rapport we have with a person, the more we will be able to achieve. A deeper relationship is many times stronger than a shallow one. Connection is everything.

Step 6: Connection

In summary

- Connect with people through what you talk about and with non-verbal rapport.

- Remember: about seven percent of the meaning of what we say is conveyed in the words themselves. The rest of the message is in our voice and other non-verbal communication.

- Help the natural building of rapport by matching with:
  - Your posture, movement, and gestures
  - Your breathing
  - Your voice

- On meeting resistance from other people, build more rapport.

- Rapport is a precious commodity; look after it.

- Connect with people at a deeper level—from the heart—for a lasting connection.

Relating to you

- With whom will you make new and deeper connections?

- What's the biggest learning you have taken from this chapter?

Step 7:
Values

Working the levers of progress

Before *You may:*	**After** *You will:*
✗ Be unsure how to get someone's interest	✔ Move quickly to find out what matters to people
✗ Struggle to convince people of the merits of a proposal	✔ Have a shorthand way of remembering what defines the individuals you meet
✗ Be unclear about your own values and how they determine your behaviour	✔ Be able to sell an idea or product or gather support for a proposal
✗ Find all the different issues in play confusing and hard to work with effectively	✔ Get other people to do what you and they want while letting them think it was their idea in the first place
✗ Sense that something is blocking a relationship you are trying to build	✔ Be able to build coalitions around a common purpose
✗ Fail to spot the unmet needs that are driving behaviour	✔ Understand the sequence in which people are likely to try and satisfy their needs
	✔ Know how to deal with the key unmet need

Step 7: Values

Fulfilling values and meeting unmet needs are the keys to progress with other people. If we find out what others want, offer a way to help them, and then deliver on our promises, they will help us with what we want. Even if we are unable to give them anything concrete, just respecting their wishes will help our relationship. We can get to know someone very well by finding out what they see as important, and that small amount of information can summarise what drives a person. Our day-to-day experience of them is then just details.

Organising around values

Our values are revealed by how we spend our time. What we do minute-to-minute reflects what we see as important, whether consciously or unconsciously. That behaviour is just the tip of the iceberg—the part of what we do that is visible, influenced underneath the surface by our skills and capabilities, beliefs and values, and sense of identity. Our identity is, in turn, shaped by larger entities of which we are part, such as countries and organisations, our connectedness to something bigger than ourselves, and ultimately some kind of spiritual context, with or without organised religion.

Our observable behavior

Our skills and capabilities

Our beliefs and values

Our identity or sense of self

The larger systems that shape our identity
(e.g. nationality, gender, religion, organisations)

A natural hierarchy links the levels of the "iceberg," and if we turn it the other way up, we arrive at the "Neurological Levels Model" developed by Robert Dilts from earlier work by Gregory Bateson.

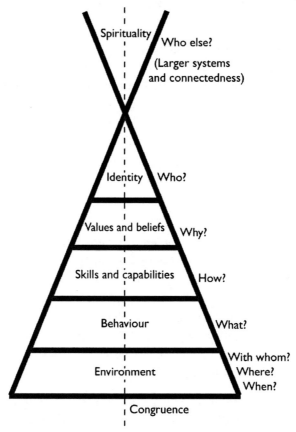

Starting second from bottom, our "behaviour" is what we do and what other people see us doing—activities they could describe with verbs. The level below is the "environment" in which we exist and act—where, when, and with whom. As Tad James and Wyatt Woodsmall point out, "The highest quality information is behavioural," in the sense that we can describe it accurately. The levels higher up involve progressively more consequential but less precise information. Moving up the hierarchy to the third level, "skills and capabilities" refers to the techniques and strategies by which we organise our behaviour to achieve what we want or value, drawing on our beliefs about how the world works. Values and beliefs appear at the fourth level and, in turn, are a reflection of our sense of identity—who we are—which is at the top of the pyramid, the fifth level. Above that, the model hints at the influence of spiritual beliefs or more prosaic organisational and national cultures of which we are part.

By asking appropriate open questions, we can use this model as a template to gather information about another person, working our way up the levels.

With good rapport, we can do this even on first meeting, deepening the relationship quickly.

As a father (part of my identity), I value what's good for my children both now and in the future, and I have beliefs about what actions will fit with that. Those beliefs may or may not be valid. Nevertheless, that's what I work with, using my skills as best I can to achieve the things that I believe will support my children. These skills result in behaviour that the family might actually see around the home, such as asking about their schoolwork or going out to work for an income to provide for their needs. In a reflective moment, I might ponder the spiritual significance and privilege of having children and wonder if I am up to the calling.

The notion of "congruence" is important—the extent to which the levels in the hierarchy are aligned and supportive of each other. If our skills and capabilities, our behaviour and our environment truly reflect our identity and our values and beliefs, then we will be at ease with ourselves and come across that way to other people. Our energy levels will be high and we will seem capable and grounded. As Robert Dilts said, "When somebody is completely congruent, all kinds of things can be going wrong in the world, and he can handle it very well. But if somebody is incongruent and in conflict with himself, any little thing can cause stress."

If what we are doing is poorly aligned with our values, our energy will be drained by internal conflict, and we will be much less effective in what we do and in our interactions with other people. We will come across as not knowing our own mind and unclear about what we want.

If the work we do lacks integrity for us, then we, the work, and the people we do it with will suffer. Parker J. Palmer

Achieving congruence at all times is a challenge and something to be worked toward. I experience tension between providing for the needs of my children now and providing for them in the future. With this incongruence, I am sometimes torn between being with them and making time for the work that will make a difference to their future security. I have found no easy solution other than to share out the time as best I can, spending some quality time with my children first, and then insisting on peace and quiet for the work I want to do, including writing this book, for example.

Because of the need to achieve or maintain congruence, changes at any one level stimulate changes at the other levels. The further up the hierarchy we go, the more influential a change at that level is. For example, we may need to work at the values level to influence behaviour—to give people "the why." The further up the hierarchy we intervene, the more impact and influence we will have. By achieving or maintaining rapport at the identity level, we can have an especially powerful discussion. For example, if I adopt a "father-to-father" approach in an appropriate way with other fathers, they may be more receptive to what I have to say than they otherwise would be.

The Neurological Levels Model can also be applied to organisations and any other groups of people with things in common such as families, cities, and countries—anywhere where the notion of "culture" is relevant. We then have a framework for considering matches and mismatches between one city and the next, for example.

Steps to take

 Pick an aspect of your life and think of the details that apply to you in that role. Where do you fulfil the role, with whom, and when? What do you do? What are the skills you are using? What are the values you hold and beliefs you draw on? What label would you apply to yourself at the identity level? How congruent or well aligned does your model seem to be? What would you change?

 When you meet somebody for the first time, rather than talking with them in an unstructured way, have the Neurological Levels Model in mind and gather information about the other person on as many levels as you can. Then you will avoid gathering many unimportant details.

Values are an especially useful level to explore because they give us the key insights we need. We will now look in more detail at how to elicit these vital bits of information.

Discovering values

Values are the key to understanding what makes a person do what they do. Provided we have a sufficient level of rapport, we can find out someone's values by asking:

What's important to you about _____? *or*
What do you like in a _____? *or*
What do you get out of _____?

Here we complete the question with the context we are interested in or whatever the other person has just been talking about. Typically, we will get two or three values. We can then follow up with:

What else is important to you about _____? *or just*
What else?

We may then get two or three more values, ending up with about five in total. Two questions are enough; any more could be intrusive. Despite asking in a specific context, we'll often be able to infer something about the person's values more broadly from their answers. If we want general information and the circumstances are appropriate, we can ask directly:

What's important to you in life?

Or if it's clear from the context or our tone that we're asking a general question:

What's important to you?

We need an appropriately high level of rapport to ask these questions.

Things get a little more complicated because people may not be consciously aware of their more deeply held "core" values. For example, most adults would be appalled to see children coming to harm, but probably wouldn't mention this if "stopped on the street" and asked what their values were. Yet when they see a picture of a starving child, they'll have a strong response just the same. We need to observe somebody's behaviour to decide what values are really in charge. Over time, people's actions don't lie.

Values held unconsciously can often be more important than those expressed. Sometimes we get into difficulty because at the conscious level, we share a value with another person, but at an unconscious level, we are conflicted. We may find it difficult to discuss these things because the other person isn't consciously aware of what's driving their behaviour either. They might not even realise there is a conflict.

From the example file

 A family agreed on a plan for a day out to visit a museum. The father unconsciously valued the time together as a family unit. The mother did too, but even more wanted a break from the pressures of work. When they arrived, they found a special event taking place, making the museum a busy and noisy place. Unexpectedly, they had an argument about whether to go ahead with the visit because she didn't think their experience would be very peaceful and he didn't understand why that was important to her.

The values people tell us they have may only be what they think they are supposed to see as important in their roles at home or work. They may feel that we will disapprove if they tell us that the real reason they want something is to beat their rival to a promotion, for example. In organisations, individuals may have values that are very different from what the corporate entity claims its values to be. An organisation's true values are revealed by what its people do rather than what the corporate brochure says. If an organisation says that one of its values is service and its customers are routinely kept waiting, then something else is more important.

Steps to take

 Take opportunities to find out about people's values by asking them what's important to them in what they're doing or what they're talking about. You'll take strides ahead by making this a habit, because few do this. You'll leave a short conversation with an idea of what would please a person while the rest just had a chat.

We waste our time if we expect people to behave in ways that are not aligned with their values. It just won't happen with any consistency. You can save yourself a great deal of time and energy by recognising this reality. People devote their time to what they see as important and make their decisions accordingly.

Values in relationships

The higher up the hierarchy of levels we can relate to someone, the deeper the relationship will be. When we meet someone for the first time, we find common ground at the lower levels and then gradually move up as we gain confidence in the relationship. In particular, finding out a person's or organisation's values—and making good use of that information—will enable a relationship to move forward much more quickly. We are in a position to offer them what they want.

I have had feedback that I get other people to do what I want while letting them think that it was their idea in the first place, even in complex situations. I don't set out with that in mind, but that is the apparent effect of discovering their values and then finding ways to match them with my proposal. The approach is effective in bringing a disparate group of people together in support of a common objective. If they didn't support the proposal at some level, the approach wouldn't work, so I am acting in their interest.

When selling something—cars, say—finding out what the customer wants in a car and then showing them only the models that match those values is likely to be a good approach. The principle also applies when we're selling other things.

We can use the Neurological Levels Model in an interpersonal or interorganisational context to explore areas of similarity and areas of difference, with a view to acknowledging both. If we find conflict at a lower level of the model—at the behaviour level, for example—we may be able to overcome this by working at a higher level, such as the values level. We can resolve disputes by demonstrating that, while we may be in conflict at a lower level, at a higher level we have things in common. Defining, debating, and even just talking about values, however, can be difficult because the language used is often very general and abstract. Values are expressed by words such as "safety," "honesty," and "integrity," which are known as "nominalisations" and involve labels being applied to actions. Two people may claim to hold the same values and yet act very differently in similar situations because their understanding of the words is quite different.

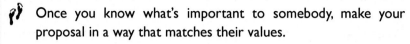

Climbing a staircase of needs

Of all the things others may value, chances are just one of them will be the driver of their behaviour at any given moment. Abraham Maslow's "Hierarchy of Needs"—another model with levels—may give us a clue as to what that might be:

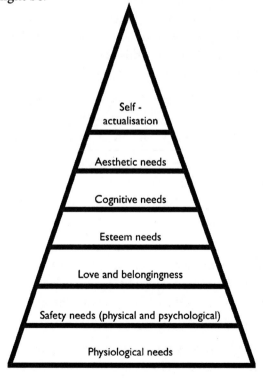

Maslow argued that we only seek to satisfy a need at a particular level if all our needs at the lower levels are already met. Our motivation will come from the lowest unsatisfied level in the hierarchy. Maslow's Hierarchy of Needs is often applied to the long-term motivation of employees, but if we look at our own and others' behaviour during any one day, we can see that we move up and down the levels minute-to-minute.

We begin each day at the lowest level, attending to our physiological needs—food, drink, air to breathe, sleep, and so on. We deal next with our need for both physical and psychological safety. Our physical safety may not be too much of an issue unless we live in a war zone or an extreme climate, but our psychological safety could be at risk in the sense that we may feel insecure about something.

Assuming we do feel safe, we move on to affiliating with other people and acting as part of a group with family, friends, or co-workers. We give and receive trust, acceptance, love, and affection as appropriate. We build rapport. The resulting belongingness gives us the possibility of meeting our esteem needs through the respect of both others and ourselves.

If we are physiologically satisfied, feel safe, belong to a group, and have a measure of self-esteem, only then do we operate effectively at the cognitive level in which we seek knowledge, understanding, meaning, and predictability. In the work context, this is the level we need to reach to be attentive to anything other than the most repetitive of work tasks.

Once all is in order at the thinking level, we then seek beauty, symmetry, balance, order, and form in art and nature, perhaps by attending a concert or engaging in some other leisure pursuit involving aesthetically pleasing things.

Finally, if we climb all the way to the top level, we may be able to "self-actualise" by fully expressing ourselves and becoming all we are capable of becoming. We may struggle to make it all the way up to self-actualisation on any given day and may get stuck trying to fulfil a need at one of the lower levels.

At the end of each day, we come back down the hierarchy, finally attending to our need for rest. We can be brought low by illness, threats to our physical or psychological safety, and instability in our relationships. If we are ill, for example, we are reduced to trying to fulfil our needs at the bottom level of the hierarchy and everything above may have to be forgotten.

We might also be moving up the levels when something happens in our dealings with other people, and we suddenly feel threatened by a break in rapport. An example would be being overruled or put down in a meeting. We may feel hurt at the esteem and belonging levels and drop back to needing to meet our need for security again as we "lose face." The effect is like climbing a staircase and sometimes falling down:

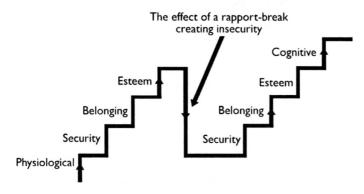

Maslow's model and relationships

Relationship needs are an integral part of Maslow's Hierarchy, appearing at the third level and so a key enabler for everything above. Little will be achieved without satisfactory relationships. Improving our skill with people is likely to help us spend more of our time at the higher levels.

Unmet needs drive emotion and behaviour, and we can usefully explore what those unmet needs might be when we notice behaviour that stands out. As William Ury suggests: "Treat your emotions as signposts, pointing at your core needs." So which levels of the hierarchy do we think are satisfied and which are not? Figuring out which level people are trying to satisfy at any given time can help us interact with them. For example, there is little point trying to establish a relationship with someone if their physical needs are not met.

Steps to take

 When you are speaking to someone, perhaps someone you don't have dealings with every day, practise assessing which level you think they are on. To do this, it will help you to memorise the levels of Maslow's model.

We know from experience that problems with partners can distract people from their work. Maslow's Hierarchy shows us why this is all but inevitable. If the belonging need is unmet, full attention to higher levels is going to be elusive. If my belonging need gets muddled, I have great difficulty sustaining my efforts on the higher levels, such as learning, working, and so on, even though I need this to earn a living. Much that I have built up may be at risk of crashing down. Interfering with relationship foundations can be very expensive.

Working at the esteem level through our relationships can help us move further up the hierarchy. Self-esteem comes from closing the gap between our self-image and our ideal self (i.e., the difference between the person we want to be and the person we think we actually are). If the gap is large, we have low self-esteem. If the gap is small, we have high self-esteem. People with high self-esteem tend to attract other people and so build relationships easily.

Developing our self-awareness involves refining our self-image so that it is closer to how other people see us, and this may bring it closer to our ideal self-concept because we are often our own harshest critic. At the same time, accepting that some aspects of our ideal self are not that important and letting go of them can bring our ideal self-concept down toward our self-image and increase our self-esteem that way too.

Steps to take

 How can you reorganise your life and your environment with Maslow's Hierarchy in mind, so that you spend more of your time at the higher levels?

The key unmet need

One particular unmet need crops up so frequently that it's almost a constant factor in our lives. That unmet need is the need for psychological security. People feel scared a lot of the time, even though things usually turn out all right. The consequences of fear dominate our lives, families, and organisations.

My life was full of terrible events, most of which never happened.
George Bernard Shaw

Fear has its place and sometimes a bit of insecurity is needed to get people moving, especially in a crisis, but too much can paralyse a person or an organisation. As Stephen Covey said: "Next to physical survival, the greatest need of a human being is psychological survival—to be understood, to be affirmed, to be validated, to be appreciated. And after that vital need is met, you can then focus on influencing or problem solving."

If we're having difficulty building a relationship with someone and they seem indifferent to our efforts, that may well indicate an unmet need for security. Until the other person feels secure, our efforts at relationship-building are pointless. Of course, we may not be the cause or the only cause of the feeling of insecurity. Nevertheless, the question is: What can we do to put the other person at ease?

Steps to take

 If you're not succeeding with somebody, it's likely that they are feeling insecure about something. What could that be and what can you do about it? What is the reassurance you could provide?

We waste our time if we try to build relationships or work on an issue with people if they feel physically or mentally insecure. The first of these is obvious enough, but consciously taking steps to promote people's mental security is not so often done and is, therefore, a major opportunity. Unmet need for security—fear—is a far bigger driver in what happens around us and in our lives than we typically realise. If we recognise and deal with unmet needs for security, we can really move ahead because so few people do that. Most are so busy trying to attend to their own insecurities that they have no time for anyone else's, but attending to others' needs for security is a great way to meet our own. We get back what we put out, of course.

From the example file

 When we arrive at a public gathering, we tend to avoid sitting in the front row. We have an unmet need for mental security, which we seek to meet by sitting somewhere farther back, surrounded by others, where we feel safe from being asked a question or having some other dreadful thing happen to us.

Many large organisations and the people within them have a surprisingly high need for security, which shows up as an aversion to risk. If they behave as if they have an unmet need for security, what does that say about their effectiveness at the higher levels of Maslow's Hierarchy? In organisations, senior people can be just as fearful as more junior staff. The fear may relate to a different threat, but the emotion is the same and just as debilitating.

Steps to take

- Notice when people behave in a way that suggests they feel insecure. What can you do to help them feel safe? If you can do this effectively, people will respond well to you and treat you as a leader.

- If other people's security and self-esteem needs are met, take great care to avoid disrupting them by an inappropriate remark, unless you really mean to shake their foundations. If you do, be aware that you will need to wait some time before they are ready to engage again at higher levels. Stability around security and self-esteem needs is precious. Look after it.

- As a host or organiser of an event, taking steps to reassure people that their mental security will not be disrupted can go a long way to getting the event flowing. Provided that you reassure people they will not be picked on, they will be happy to accept your invitation to move down to the front rather than congregate at the back.

If we attend to other people on the level they are currently, we will get along well with them, and a high level of rapport will develop quickly. If on the other hand, we address them at too high a level, we may seem presumptuous. They are likely to seem distracted to us and attempt to disengage in order to focus on getting their lower level needs met. When we leave someone stuck at a low level, everything we do with them after that may well be unsuccessful.

When you work with values and needs

Knowing what's important to the people in your life and work is the easy way to make progress. If you're clear about what they want, you can work out how to help them get it in a way that works for you too. A little thought given to the best order in which to address people's needs will help, as will being sensitive to the ubiquitous unmet need for security.

Step 7: Values

In summary

📄 Values determine how we spend our time and are a useful indicator for what drives a person.

📄 Discovering someone's values is the key to making progress with them.

📄 Maslow's Hierarchy of Needs can help us understand what may be the key driver for a person at any given time.

📄 An unmet need for mental security is often a debilitating and dominant driver in a situation. What can we do to provide reassurance?

Relating to you

📄 Whose values and needs could you do with understanding better?

📄 What are you going to do differently after reading this chapter?

Step 8: Language

Unwinding the issues

Before *You may:*	**After** *You will:*
✗ Miss opportunities to resolve problems by not questioning what people say	✔ Be familiar with the deletions, generalisations, and distortions that occur in everyday speech
✗ Contribute to problems yourself with your language	✔ Spot the patterns of language others use
✗ Be unaware that certain linguistic patterns point to issues that can be worked on	✔ Notice your own patterns
	✔ Be able to unwind the effect of imprecise language
	✔ Have tools to work with in any problem situation
	✔ Use language in a way that helps you communicate clearly and without confrontation

Step 8: Language

How useful would it be to have a system of language skills that would give you something to work with in any problem situation? The "Meta-model" that lies at the heart of NLP does just that. You can use it without having to be creative in the moment. If someone says A, you ask B; if they say C, you ask D; if they say E, you ask F; and so on. These questions will often be all it takes to get a problem unstuck. They're great when you're under pressure because you don't really need to think that much to use them. With practice, they can easily be an unconscious competence.

Issues in relationships often stem from inadequacies in the way we express ourselves. We may be lazy in the way we use our vocabulary, or we may exaggerate, or the words we say may incompletely represent what we mean. Even what we mean to say may inaccurately reflect our thoughts. Other people respond to what we say rather than what we think, of course, and we can be confused ourselves about the things we say to others. Being precise in our language can sometimes be all that is required to resolve a problem.

Richard Bandler and John Grinder gathered a systematic approach for working with the patterns in the things we say, drawing on the field of linguistics and the techniques used by the "wizards" they studied: "While the techniques of these wizards are different, they share one thing: They introduce changes in their client's models which allow their clients more options in their behaviour. Each of these wizards has a map or model for changing their client's models of the world—i.e., a Meta-model—which allows them to effectively expand and enrich their clients' models in some way that makes the client's lives richer and more worth living." This linguistic aspect of NLP is based on Alfred Korzybski's work on semantics, combined with Noam Chomsky's syntactic theory of transformational grammar.

One of the great strengths of the Meta-model is that it provides comprehensive coverage of the opportunities to intervene that are evident in the language we use. There is always something we can do. The system is prescriptive in its approach: if the client says this, then we ask that; if the client says the other, then we ask the appropriate question for that pattern.

Typically, repeated instances or patterns appear in what people say, especially when things are difficult for them in their relationships. Often, "deletions," "generalisations," and "distortions" fuel the developing tension or crisis in a relationship when, at a deeper level, there is less conflict. The actual problem is much smaller than the apparent problem. Using the Meta-model can not only reduce the apparent size of the problem, but also create momentum toward a solution. The technique takes a bit of learning and practice, but the gains are well worth it. You will easily recoup the time invested.

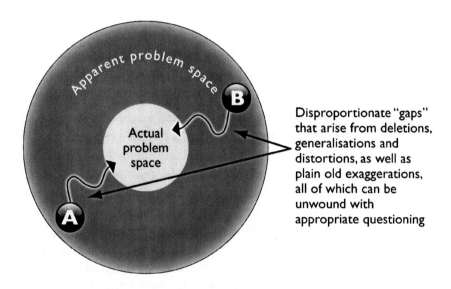

How the Meta-model system works

The Meta-model recognises the way we organise our models of the world. In order to cope with the amount of information we receive, we adjust what we take in to fit with what we already know. We delete bits, generalise beliefs, and distort what happens so that we can add to our model of the world. This is a very effective process and enables us to deal with great complexity.

Just as we delete, generalise, and distort information on the way into our model, we distort, generalise, and delete information on the way out, so our spoken and written language is only an approximation of what's in our head. The imprecision in what we say, though apparently insignificant, can be the cause of many problems, and so it also provides a rich source of opportunity for change.

We can define three levels of information:

Surface Structure What we say outwardly to other people (and inwardly to ourselves) in our native language—English, for example.

Deep Structure What we would say if we used a semantically complete, linguistically "well-formed" sentence—one that is not just grammatically correct, but has all the necessary elements for meaning. The deep structure may include information that does not make it into the surface structure of what we actually say.

Reference Structure Even if we say something that is semantically complete, it might still be a defective description of the model we hold in our VAK representational systems, which is our reference structure.

Much of our model of the world is coded, not in our native language, but in terms of basic sensory information. That is the reference structure. For example, our ability to walk is coded in a mixture of visual and kinaesthetic representations with a little auditory thrown in, so if we want to describe how we use our legs to go upstairs, we will need to convert the sensory process associated with lifting our feet into a linguistic form. We probably would find that difficult to do in a comprehensive way, describing every muscle movement. However, most of us can climb stairs without problems, proving that we have an effective reference structure (or strategy) coded in sensory terms. (The reference structure is also the basis of our non-verbal communication.)

During the process of transformation from reference structure to deep structure and then surface structure as we speak, information may be deleted, generalised, and distorted. We do this all the time to make our communication efficient, so spoken and written language is full of these features.

The purpose of the Meta-model is to notice the deletions, distortions, and generalisations that may not be helping us, treat them as signposts to issues, and recover the information in the deep structure.

We can access the missing information through a system of questions or "challenges" indicated by the specific pattern we notice. The questions in the sections that follow make the deep structure explicit. Working in rapport is vital, or the person being questioned is liable to feel challenged or brought up short.

To use the Meta-model, listen to what the other person is saying until you notice one of the patterns that seems to be causing a problem—blocking the person somehow. Then interrupt gently with the appropriate question— one that corresponds to the pattern you noticed. The other person will stop to answer or think about your question, then carry on with a modified train of thought. Wait for the next feature that it seems helpful to challenge, and so on. You can, of course, notice your own patterns and challenge yourself to break down problems of your own. Some deletions, generalisations, and distortions are helpful, though, so take care to work only on the ones that are associated with the problem or "stuck state."

Here, we'll assume that the Meta-model patterns are arising in speech, but they could also be in written language. Some of the patterns have labels with linguistic terms, which we will use because they help make the system clear. I've indicated an informal name in brackets as well in these cases.

Deletions are the simplest to understand, so we'll start with them.

Deletions

We tend to use words imprecisely or omit them altogether. There are five categories of deletion and in each case, a specific type of question will lead to the missing information.

Simple Deletions

In a simple deletion, something is left out of a sentence, leaving the listener unsure of what is meant, and even the speaker may be unclear as to precisely what they had in mind. The question recovers the missing part.

I am mystified.	*Mystified about what, specifically?*
I don't agree.	*With what or whom?*
I can't.	*Can't do what, exactly?*
I am going to work on it tomorrow.	*What exactly is "it?"*

Very commonly, we refer to "it" without being clear to the listener, or even ourselves sometimes, what "it" is. Encouraging the speaker to explain what "it" is can often greatly aid understanding. We can use a question such as the one above, referring to "it" with appropriate emphasis.

Comparative Deletions

We sometimes leave out the criterion of a comparison, and this may be recovered with an appropriate question.

The project is better.	*Better than what, specifically?*
We have fewer customer complaints.	*Fewer than what (or when)?*
The department is doing better.	*Better than what, specifically?*
That's expensive.	*Compared with what?*

This last example is very useful in sales when the customer may not be making a like-for-like comparison. Sometimes potential buyers object to the price asked in a habitual way without really believing that the price is expensive. The question will reveal that when the comparison is made properly, the objection falls away.

Sometimes the criterion of the comparison does appear in a separate sentence: "It's wet and windy today. The weather will be better tomorrow." Taken together, the meaning is clear and there is no need to question the statement.

Unspecified Referential Index (Vague Subjects)

Sometimes the grammatical subjects of our sentences don't identify the individuals we are talking about (the "referential index" in linguistic terminology). This imprecision can fuel conflict and stop us finding solutions, so we can ask a question to clarify to whom the statement is referring.

People don't let you make decisions.	*Which people, specifically?*
Managers can't be trusted.	*Which managers can't be trusted?*
People just don't learn.	*Which people, specifically?*

Usually the speaker is thinking of particular individuals when making these statements even though, until pressed, they won't identify them, either because they haven't made the effort to express themselves fully or are reluctant to "name names." In either case, the statements with unspecified subjects fuel a vague feeling of tension that no one can do much about, because they don't have the specifics to work with.

Unspecified Verbs (Vague Verbs)

Here, "unspecified" means inadequately defined. Sometimes the verbs we use lack precision about what the subject is actually doing. Two vague verbs used often are "do" and "make." They tell us little. An appropriate question clarifies what exactly is happening or has happened.

He is going to do the floors tomorrow.	*What exactly is he going to do?*
I have difficulty communicating.	*How specifically do you have difficulty communicating?*
They have made a problem for themselves.	*What exactly have they done?*
He went to Chicago yesterday.	*How specifically did he go?*

As always, uncertainty about meaning can cause problems. Vague verbs can be refined with appropriate questioning.

Nominalisations (Abstractions)

Nominalisations are very common, especially in organisational life, and can endanger accurate communication and working relationships. Nominalisations arise when actions (verbs) are turned into things or events (nouns). If a noun is not a physical thing, it's a nominalisation, often ending in "-ment" or "-tion." Using nominalisations can have the effect of disempowering the speaker from engaging with and influencing what is, in fact, an ongoing process.

The trouble with a nominalisation is some of the meaning is lost and misinterpretation can result. Here are some examples and the kind of things they might mean, defined by two different people:

Empowerment	*Staff feeling that they have some control, or Having enough information or skills to take charge of a situation and not needing to rely on others to help come to decisions*
Employee engagement	*Staff interacting with managers, or Feeling connected with a role and motivated*
Decision	*Coming to a point of view, or Selecting from a number of options*
Contribution	*Doing something to help, or Adding to the bottom line*

You may well define these words differently and not agree with any version. That's the point. Nominalisations mean different things to different people—often they mean what people want them to mean, which might not be what we had in mind. Values are expressed as nominalisations (such as "service," "honesty," and "trust") and can be difficult to discuss effectively. Using nominalisations can make business or any other writing impenetrable and tiring to read. (They are used on purpose in hypnosis to confuse and distract the conscious mind.)

Questions can put the action or "activity" that has been distorted into an "object" back into a process statement.

We need more empowerment.	What kind of empowerment?
I don't like the decision they have made.	What are they deciding about?
The relationship is over.	Who was relating to whom about what and in what way?

"Manipulation" is also, of course, a nominalisation, which goes some way to explaining why we struggle to decide whether NLP (or anything else) is or isn't manipulative. The word means different things to different people. So long as we continue using a nominalisation, we'll never settle the matter.

Our language will be more powerful and more action-oriented if we use verbs and reduce the nominalisations in our language. If we want to be sure to maintain or build rapport with someone, however, the vagueness of nominalisations is useful.

From the example file

 One evening, our son with autism was trying to interact with his older brother (who is very caring toward his younger sibling). My wife said, "Give him some attention," and the older boy looked round, puzzled. Because of the nominalisation in the request, he didn't know what he was expected to do.

Generalisations

Generalisations arise from limitations in a person's model of the world and can block progress toward solutions. There are three types.

Universal Quantifiers (Universal Statements)

Sometimes we state things as being universally true as a broad generalisation, using words such as "always," "never," "all," "every," or "no one." To challenge this, we can look for a counter-example to demonstrate that the generalisation is untrue.

She is always critical of me.	*Always? Has there ever been a time when she wasn't?*
No one ever takes me seriously.	*No one? Ever?*
She never listens.	*Never?*

We also sometimes make statements without using the universal words themselves, but still exclude the possibility of exceptions. (This book is full of such sentences, because it would be tedious if I always qualified what I say to indicate that the statement may not apply in every single case.) We can notice such universal statements and challenge them if they are the source of a problem.

I wash the dishes in our household.	*Does no one else wash the dishes in your household?*
Men like to drive fast.	*Do all men like to drive fast?*

Avoid making a universal statement that may be an unhelpful generalisation.

Modal Operators of Necessity (Drivers)

This category has a complicated-sounding name, but is easy to understand. We have patterns where we allude to rules of behaviour using "should," "need," "must," "have to," and "ought to," for example, when in fact, we are making choices. The patterns reflect a tendency to "blame" the world rather than recognise choice and take responsibility for what we decide. We can question this to highlight the "consequence" that has caused the rule to be created and imply that it is a cost that might be borne. The speaker will then notice that they are making a choice.

I have to learn this material.	*What would happen if you didn't?*
She has to visit her mother.	*What would happen if she didn't?*
You must follow the rules.	*What would happen if I didn't?*
I need to do the shopping	*What would happen if you didn't?*

With an awareness of this pattern in ourselves, we might choose to replace "I need to" with "I want to" or "I have decided to" in order to re-associate ourselves with the choice we have made. Then we will feel more in control and seem more balanced to other people. If we have a pattern of being "driven" by external factors, we can be difficult to be around. (I know; that's one of my traits.)

From the example file

 A prominent, if slightly trivial, example of this pattern is when we use the filler words: "I have to say…" The effect is to imply that we have no choice but to open our mouths and speak, as if we are not in command of our bodies. The result is we dissociate from our remark and diminish our personal presence. It's better to stand behind what we say and take responsibility for it. If you don't want to be responsible for your words, don't say them.

Modal Operators of Possibility (Stoppers and Limiters)

Aspects of our models of the world limit our behaviour. We perceive these to be absolute barriers, but in fact, they are a reflection of choices we have made. The purpose of a challenge is to identify the actual cause of the problem and highlight to the subject that they are in fact making, or have made, a choice.

I'd like to, but I can't.	*What stops you?*
It's just not possible.	*Suppose it were possible. How might it happen?*
I can't learn this material.	*What stops you?*
I can't apologize.	*What actually stops you apologizing?*

Unlocking the limiting beliefs implicit in these statements can go a long way to resolving issues.

Distortions

There are five types of distortions.

Complex Equivalence (Interpretation)

The speaker uses a pattern that suggests that "this" means "that" in an objective sense, when in fact it is an expression of part of their model of the world. Challenging such a pattern checks the validity of the implied relationship and highlights its subjective nature.

He's performing poorly in school. He has a learning problem.	*How does his performing poorly in school mean he has a learning problem?*
You're not speaking to me. You're upset.	*How does me not speaking to you mean that I am upset?*
You're not smiling. You're obviously not enjoying yourself.	*How does the fact I am not smiling mean I am not enjoying myself?*

Our models of the world include many beliefs in the form of complex equivalences. Most of them serve us well, but some don't. Those are the ones to challenge.

Presuppositions

We need to know something implicitly to understand a statement. Questioning can recover the missing presuppositions.

If he knew how much I suffered, he wouldn't keep acting in that way.	*How are you suffering?* *How is he acting?* *How do you know he doesn't know?*

We can spot three presuppositions in the original statement here: "I suffer," "He acts in some way," and "He doesn't know I suffer." The questions clarify the unspecified verbs "suffer" and "act" and highlight the complex equivalence in "He acts in that way: He doesn't know I suffer." The speaker's intention is for the listener to accept the presuppositions as true, without discussion, even though the distortion may well be causing problems in the relationship. Another example is the salesperson's question, "Would you like a red one or a green one?" which presupposes that you want one.

Cause—Effect (Blamers)

In a "cause—effect" construction, there is an implied causal link between a particular stimulus and response, through which blame is attached when there is no real, physical causal link. We are not, in fact, able to impose an emotion on another human being. The purpose of the challenge is to identify the causal links implied in the statement and highlight to the subject that they do, in fact, have control of their response and can take responsibility if they choose.

She makes me so angry.	*How specifically does she make you angry?*
This company drives me mad.	*How does the company drive you mad?*

With the question, we intend the speaker to notice that they are, in fact, choosing their response.

Some cause—effect patterns are helpful, especially in the family context. For example, "My husband makes me feel wonderful whenever he looks at me that way." We would not want to challenge this "glue" that holds the family together.

Mind-reading

In "mind-reading," people claim to know someone else's internal thoughts or experience, which, of course, they can only guess. The challenge has the effect of highlighting that the subject does not, in fact, have knowledge of another's thoughts.

He doesn't care about me.	*How do you know he doesn't care about you?*
I know why you did that.	*How do you know that?*
She's only saying that to hurt me.	*How do you know that?*

Mind-reading causes much interpersonal difficulty and communication breakdown, particularly between partners and family members. Challenging mind-reading is an important part of developing communication in a family system. It also reveals to family members just how much their "map is not the territory."

In some circumstances, it can be useful to attempt to mind-read, but only if we recognise that our ability to do so successfully is limited.

Lost Performative (Opinions Stated as Facts)

This form of distortion involves the statement of opinions (value judgments) as if they are facts. The appropriate question re-associates the value judgment with the speaker and identifies the criteria used to make the judgment.

It's selfish to think of your own feelings.	*Selfish according to whom?*
This is the way to do the job.	*According to whom?*
It's very unprofessional.	*According to whom?*
He should go and speak to his wife.	*Who thinks he should go and speak to his wife?*

A well-formed version of these statements would start something like: "I think that it's selfish to..." or "I believe he should..."—then the speaker "owns" the opinion expressed. The absence of the ownership is what's meant by the term "lost performative." If we do want to express an opinion, especially a challenging one, we will come across much more effectively if we start with: "I think you should..." than if we start with: "You should...." With the former, we're putting our personal credibility behind the statement, rather than implying some universal truth.

Unwinding issues using the Meta-model

You can use the system of Meta-model questions both on yourself and in your relationships with other people. The patterns pop up all over the place in everyday conversation. The first step is to start noticing them. Next, if you have the necessary rapport, you can ask appropriate questions to work on the issues that the patterns highlight. In coaching, the usual approach is to look out for the patterns of speech being used by the client in a context that seems to be associated with their issue, especially when that pattern is repeated.

A single sentence may contain more than one pattern, such as a deletion and a distortion. If more than one is evident, it doesn't greatly matter which you tackle first. Go for the one that seems most deep-seated in the other person's thinking. Formal coaching would deal with distortions first, then generalisations to explore limiting thinking, and finally deletions, but start with whatever feature seems to be most fundamental to the issue.

In using the Meta-model, take care to leave in place the deletions, generalisations, and distortions that are useful to you or the other person. For example, family systems depend for their stability on complex equivalences such as: "He brings me flowers. I know he cares." Focus on the areas that are unhelpful.

In sales, if the customer says, "Once I have the proof, I can place an order," which is an example of cause—effect, leave the distortion alone and ask, "What proof do you need?"

Aside from the business applications, I have found the Meta-model to be particularly useful in helping my children overcome problems they have and express themselves clearly.

Steps to take

👣 Make some flash cards with all the example statements given in this chapter on one side, one per card, and the appropriate questions on the reverse, along with the category of that example (3 x 5 cards would be suitable). Then look at each statement in turn and test yourself on the style of question that is appropriate. Learn the categories as well because that will increase your familiarity with the systematic approach.

👣 Write a few paragraphs about a problem you have or record yourself speaking. Look for Meta-model patterns in what you have said and challenge yourself about them. How does that change your thinking about the issue?

👣 Practise with a friend. Take turns talking about an issue of your own and see what Meta-model patterns you notice. Ask appropriate questions and see what develops from them.

👣 Start looking out for Meta-model patterns in the conversations you have. You might find it easier to focus on just some of the categories to begin with.

👣 Once you have developed some familiarity with the patterns, you can turn your attention to other people's use of them. Challenge patterns you recognise when they come up and you sense it would be useful to do so. Remember: establish good rapport and be careful with your tone of voice. You might want to use "softening" words such as "I wonder if I could ask…" or "I'm curious to know…" with your question. You might also want to say at the outset that part of your role is to ask questions that haven't been asked before or something along those lines that fits your context.

👣 Work on reducing the number of nominalisations and lost performatives (disowned opinions) you use in your written and spoken language. Expand this self-improvement to include the other patterns.

The great thing about the Meta-model is that it always gives you something to work with in a problem situation. Always? Pretty much, I reckon.

A summary of the Meta-model

Each category of Meta-model pattern is listed with an example and the appropriate challenge:

Category	Example	Challenge
Deletions		
Simple Deletion	I don't agree.	*With what specifically?*
Comparative Deletion	That's expensive.	*Compared with what?*
Unspecified Referential Index	People just don't listen.	*Who specifically doesn't listen?*
Unspecified Verb	He is doing the floors.	*What is he doing?*
Nominalisation	We need more communication.	*How are we going to communicate?*
Generalisations		
Universal Quantifier	He always shouts at me.	*Always?*
Modal Operator of Necessity	I have to finish this.	*What would happen if you didn't?*
Modal Operator of Possibility	I can't.	*What stops you?*
Distortions		
Complex Equivalence	You're not speaking to me. You're upset.	*How does my not speaking to you mean I'm upset?*
Presupposition	If he knew how much I suffered, he wouldn't act in that way.	*How are you suffering? How is he acting? How do you know he doesn't know?*
Cause—Effect	She makes me so angry.	*How does she make you angry?*
Mind Reading	I know why you did that.	*How do you know that?*
Lost Performative	That's unprofessional.	*According to whom?*

Step 8: Language

In summary

- We delete, distort, and generalise information going from our own internal thoughts to what we actually say.

- Deletions, distortions, and generalisations can sometimes cause problems both for ourselves and for other people.

- We can identify 13 categories of deletions, distortions, and generalisations using the Meta-model from NLP and challenge them in an appropriate and systematic way (provided that we have good rapport).

- The Meta-model gives us something to work with in virtually every situation.

Relating to you

- What deletions, distortions, and generalisations might be causing you problems?

- What is the biggest learning you have taken from this chapter?

Step 9:
Self-
awareness

Seeing yourself as others see you

Before	After
You may:	*You will:*
✘ Be unaware of how you come across	✔ Explore others' points of view
✘ Be blind to traits you have that cause difficulty for other people in relating to you	✔ Have a means of assessing how you come across
✘ Ignore another person's point of view	✔ Be able to review and change your style
✘ Fail to balance your own and others' perspectives appropriately	✔ Be able to diagnose the problem when you're not getting along with someone or not achieving the results you want
✘ Repeat behaviours that are holding you back	✔ Balance your own and others' perspectives
✘ Have a self-image that isn't an accurate reflection of how others see you	✔ Be able to consider things from an observer's point of view
✘ Have low self-esteem as a result of an unrealistic ideal self or a harsh self-image (or both)	✔ Have a means of choosing your personal style for important meetings
	✔ Explore the feelings and aspirations in play with partners and family members
	✔ Bring your self-image, your ideal self, and how others see you into line

Step 9: Self-awareness

O wad some Power the giftie gie us To see oursels as ithers see us!
Robert Burns

Using a specific technique, we *can* step into the position of another person, explore their perspective, and look back at ourselves and weigh up what we see. With this heightened self-awareness, we have the option of making changes to how we come across and a greater chance of success in our relationships.

Seeing ourselves as others see us

We can use a simple but powerful process to discover things about ourselves we might never find out any other way. Other people experience our traits, but rarely tell us about them. Meanwhile, we repeat the same patterns and get the same results—some helpful, some not so helpful.

How we see ourselves and how others see us often differ in the beginning, but as we become more self-aware, we close this gap. If we are aware of how we are perceived, we have a better chance of presenting ourselves in a way that other people find interesting, friendly, and attractive. If we become aware of things we are doing that are off-putting, we can change our behaviour. Without self-awareness, we remain blind to the habits by which we undermine ourselves.

Thinking of a relationship with a specific person, you could consider the points of view of:

1. Yourself

2. The other person

3. A "fly-on-the-wall" observer

4. Specific onlookers

These four points of view or "positions" are illustrated as follows:

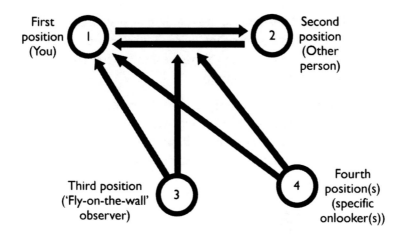

Effective relationships need a balance in these perspectives. Most of us already have some ability to think about a situation from other points of view, but we can develop these skills and be systematic and fluent in their use.

From the example file

 Martin, a business owner, was having difficulties with a staff member. With coaching, he learned to reassess the situation from his own point of view, the "problem" employee's, an unspecified observer's, and finally that of another member of staff. He realised that he was responsible for maintaining, if not causing, the problem and that by changing his behaviour, he could improve the situation. Martin found looking at things from the perspective of the real-life onlooker particularly vivid.

Shifting chairs

The process of looking at a relationship from three or more perspectives deepens our understanding of the various viewpoints, and it is the basis of an NLP technique called alternately "Perceptual Positions," "Triple Description," or "Meta-mirrors." I like to use a more informal label of "shifting chairs," which alludes to both the physical movement involved and the changes or steps in personal growth that are brought about—what some people call "shifts."

For this process, we set out chairs for the first and second position roles and move from one to the other as we consider the relationship from each viewpoint. Third position can be standing or seated, as long as it is a reasonable distance away—more than twice the distance between first and second positions. If we wish, we can also look at things from the perspective of specific onlookers (fourth position).

Using the process, we gain insights into the relationship and how we might change. Even acting on small things can make a big difference. We don't need to involve the other party at all, although we could choose to tell them what we have learned about ourselves and ask for their support in the changes we have decided to make.

The process has three or four phases:

First Position Being ourselves, visualising the other person and exploring our own viewpoint.

Second Position Sitting as the other person, looking back at ourselves from their perspective.

Third Position Moving to the position of an observer, visualising the two people and exploring that viewpoint.

Fourth Position Taking the position of a specific onlooker, again visualising the two people and exploring the real onlooker's viewpoint. This phase is optional, depending on whether real onlookers are relevant.

We can revisit positions to re-examine particular aspects if we want to or add in other perspectives.

Between each phase, we "shake off" the previous position by checking the time or counting the number of chairs in the room, for example. Loosening ourselves up physically also helps.

Within each phase the steps are similar:

1. Visualise the person opposite.

2. Notice the feelings and internal dialogue that go with the position.

3. Consider the desires and options that arise in that perspective.

4. Make suggestions for the first position role (i.e., ourselves).

The first two steps deepen our experience of that position by accessing the VAK components that go with it—to "associate" us into that position so that the things we were previously only aware of unconsciously come up. This is a necessary aspect of the process for the full benefit to be obtained. The combination of switching chairs and accessing the VAK dimensions of each position makes this process much deeper than just thinking about how somebody else might see things. We may experience strong emotions, but that means progress is being made. We are learning something.

Learning from the process

Often, the insights gained apply in a general way to all our relationships, which is a major benefit of the exercise, so the choice of specific relationship to work on is not that important. We can work on a problem relationship or in fact any relationship, including one we do not have at present, but would like to have in the future.

The effect of the process is feedback we deliver to ourselves. We can take the position of colleagues or family members and be much more direct with ourselves than they would probably be.

In first position, we can decide what we want from the other person; then, in second position, identify the behaviour from ourselves that would stimulate the desired behaviour from the other person. If these desires first come to us as a negative (i.e., something we don't want), we need to find the positive (i.e., something we do want). For example, if we start with wanting someone "not to be critical" or to "be non-judgmental," we might translate that into wanting them to be "positive," "encouraging," and "accepting."

From the example file

📂 In second position, Andy realised that to encourage a subordinate to be open, energetic, and committed, he would need to be informal and engage at a social level and that this alternative behaviour might serve him well in other relationships.

📂 Paul was struggling with his 18-month-old son making a mess with his food. When he took the position of the boy, he realised that ideas of cleanliness were unknown and that it was pointless to expect his son to abide by them. That insight is obvious to us

---

perhaps, but not to Paul, who learned to accept what he couldn't change. We often overlook such "common sense" and make difficulties for ourselves as a result. The shifting chairs process can help us rediscover these things.

I wanted to collaborate with Ian, a specialist in his field. I felt I had useful ideas but was getting nowhere. After one frustrating discussion, I sat on my own and worked through the situation. From my perspective, I wanted Ian to be receptive to my ideas. Sitting as "Ian" looking at "David," I realised that if I (David) was appreciative of what Ian was doing, then Ian would be receptive to my suggestions. Later, I told Ian about what I had learned, and he said: "That's exactly right."

Frequently, the desired behaviour is the same on both sides, and it's just a matter of who goes first. We only have control of ourselves, so if we want something different to happen, we must initiate the change.

From the example file

Peter wanted Jane to be definite in what she said. From second position, he realised that in order to get the result he wanted, he needed to be definite about what he wanted Jane to be definite about. That seems comically obvious, but it was a discovery for Peter.

Louise said she felt her estranged friend was selfish. She then realised she herself was focused on her own internal needs. Louise identified the alternative behaviour she wanted from her friend. It then dawned on her that she would only get what she wanted if she (Louise) acted first and started behaving that way toward her friend.

This example illustrates the principle of "perception is projection," which we will come to shortly. Louise saw her own selfishness in her friend.

From the observer (third) position, we may notice mismatches of various kinds. Body language and rapport may be an issue or values may be mismatched. What can we change to reduce, eliminate, or accept the mismatch? Working on rapport might be enough to resolve the situation.

From the example file

 Janice was having difficulty relating to her manager. From observer position, she could see a profound mismatch of physical and vocal energy. Janice realised that if she slowed down in her interactions with her boss, she would have a better chance of achieving rapport.

The learning from the process can often be applicable to all our relationships.

From the example file

 Angela realised she had a tendency to put herself down and that she could choose not to do that.

Sometimes, just getting in touch with the emotions the players experience can be insightful, perhaps especially for people with a strong visual or auditory preference, who may find it difficult to express their own (or others') feelings.

Shifting chairs (coaching yourself)

We can use the shifting chairs process without assistance from anyone else. We need a relaxed frame of mind and a quiet space with a couple of chairs. Here are the steps of the process written out in full. You may also find it helpful to look over the instructions that follow for the coached version. I have set out both processes in detail to make it as easy as I can for you to use them successfully.

Steps to take

1. Think of a particular relationship to work on—one that is not all it could be.

2. Imagine you are with the other person and place chairs appropriately. Decide which chair you will sit in.

First position (you)

3. Sit down in your chair (first position) and look at the person in the other chair (second position). Visualise the other person and notice the detail of how he or she looks.

4. Notice and describe your feelings (not your thoughts, your feelings). Where in your body do you experience the sensation that goes with them?

5. What are you hearing or saying to yourself?

6. Ask yourself what you want in this relationship. State your desire positively—something you want. What behaviour would you like to see from the other person?

Break state

7. Stand up and "shake off" first position by looking at something unrelated. Shaking yourself physically helps.

Second position (the other person)

8. Sit down now in the other chair in second position and visualise yourself in first position.

9. Notice and describe your feelings and sensations in second position. Where in your body do you experience them?

10. What are you hearing or saying to yourself?

11. Ask yourself, as the person in second position, what you want in this relationship. What behaviour would you like to see from the person in first position?

12. What behaviour from the person in first position would cause you to adopt the behaviour you know they want to see from you (remembered from instruction 6)?

13. What suggestion or "word in their ear" do you have for the person in first position? If you could wave a magic wand and have them do something different, what would that be?

Break state

14. Stand up and shake off second position.

Third position (an observer)

15. Move at least two or three paces away, more if space permits, to a position of an observer and visualise the two people in the relationship. Notice what you, as an observer, see as you look at them.

16. Identify and describe your feelings and sensations as an observer. Where in your body do you experience them?

17. What are you hearing or saying to yourself?
18. What do you notice about the relationship between the two people?
19. What suggestion or word in their ear do you have for the person in first position? If you could wave a magic wand and have them do something different what would that be?

Break state and review

20. Shake off observer position.
21. Review what you have learned. Consider whether these points apply generally to you, as well as to the specific relationship you are working with.

When we get to second position, we might be uncomfortable visualising ourselves in the other chair and not want to look. We might not want to "hold the mirror up." That experience in itself would tell us something important: we would be choosing not to look at what people around us see all the time. The reality is we have a real opportunity to get used to seeing ourselves from someone else's point of view, providing and receiving our own feedback, and coming to terms with ourselves.

When moving to the observer position, be sure to leave first position behind in the corresponding chair. If third position is contaminated by first position thoughts, shake off that state and move further away to a detached position as a true observer. Repeat this step if necessary. Physical distance helps. Move far enough away so that the two chairs are closer to each other than to your position as observer.

Steps to take

 Being uncomfortable seeing yourself in photographs or on video is an indication that you have something to work on. Notice you're avoiding what other people see all the time. What can you change so that you do accept what you see or can you just accept yourself as you are? Really, those are the only two options that serve you. Whether you are uncomfortable or at ease with yourself, other people will take their lead from you.

> 👣 Seek out opportunities to see and hear yourself as others do. If you find this challenging, think of it as the growth opportunity it really is. All the progress you make in accepting yourself will be reflected in the acceptance you receive from other people. Remember, you get back what you put out into the world.

Even if we're effective in our relationships most of the time, chances are we can learn something useful about ourselves using the shifting chairs process.

Shifting chairs (coaching someone else)

Being coached through the shifting chairs process can be helpful, or you might want to use the exercise with someone else. The coach should address the subject by the name appropriate to each position and use the subject's name when referring to first position. Once again, the detail is set out for your convenience.

Steps to take

1. Ask the subject to pick a particular relationship to work on and give you a name for the other person, which could be a fictional name. Let's say your subject is "Alex," and he wants to work on a relationship with a woman he refers to as "Jo."

2. Address "Alex" by name (whatever his real name is) and ask him to imagine he is with "Jo" and get him to place chairs appropriately. Have Alex decide which chair to sit in. Refer to Jo by the name Alex gives for her.

   (In the instructions that follow, replace "Alex" and "Jo" with Alex's real name and the name he or she gives for the other person.)

First position (the subject)

3. Say to Alex: "Sit down in your chair and look at Jo in the other chair. Describe what you see as you look at Jo."
   Your task here is to get Alex to visualise Jo in the other chair and for you to be convinced by what he says that he is doing that. Keep behind Alex, so that he directs his attention to the empty chair and visualises Jo sitting there. If you are in view, Alex

will just see you when he is trying to visualise Jo. If Alex turns toward you, ask him to keep looking at Jo in the other chair.

4. Now ask: "What are your feelings or emotions about Jo?" Alex may answer as if you had asked him, "What do you think about Jo?" If so, encourage him to express his feelings.

5. "Where are these feelings in you, in your body?" You want him to describe some physical sensation, and he will often indicate where with a gesture.

6. "What are you hearing or saying to yourself?"

7. "What do you want in this relationship? What would you like from Jo?"

At this point, you want Alex to express a desired behaviour, stated in a positive manner. Memorise his exact words. If he says "more" of something—"more respect," for example—suggest eliminating the word "more." Ask him if it works to say, "I want respect." (The comparative "more" weakens the process. We'll cover why in "Step 10: Attention to yourself.")

Break state

8. Ask Alex to stand up and shake off first position by focusing on something unrelated and perhaps shaking himself physically. Ask Alex what the time is, his date of birth backward, or something of that nature.

Second position (the other person)

9. "Sit down in the other chair. You are Jo now." (You will use the given name for the other person.) "Look at Alex in the other chair. Describe what you see as you look at Alex."

The task here is to get Alex to visualise himself in the other chair. You need him to see himself sitting there. Often, it helps to ask what he sees Alex wearing, which may or may not be what your subject is actually wearing as you do the exercise.

10. "What are your feelings or emotions about Alex?"

Alex may again answer as if you had asked him, "What do you think about Alex?" If so, encourage him to express the feelings that come up. He may find this difficult as this phase of the process involves a stretch, as he associates into looking back at himself. This is where much of the learning is, however, so persevere.

11. "Where in your body do you experience these feelings?"

12. "What are you hearing or saying to yourself?"

13. "What do you, Jo, want in this relationship?"

14. "What behaviour would you like to see from Alex?"

15. "Alex would like you to…." (Insert the behaviour or behaviours stated in step 7.) "What behaviour from Alex would encourage you to…?" (Again, insert the behaviour stated.)
    For example, "Alex would like respect from you. What behaviour from Alex would cause you, Jo, to show him respect?"

16. "What suggestion or 'word in their ear' do you have for Alex?"

Break state

17. Ask Alex to stand up and shake off second position.

Third position (an observer)

18. With Alex, move at least two or three paces away, ideally five or so, to a position of an interested observer. Have Alex visualise Alex and Jo in the two chairs. Ask him to describe what he sees as an observer as he looks at the two people.

    Again, your task is to get Alex to visualise the two people.

19. "What are your feelings or emotions about Alex and Jo?"

20. "Where in your body do you experience the feelings?"

21. "What are you hearing or saying to yourself?"

22. "What do you notice about the relationship between Alex and Jo?"

23. "What suggestion or 'word in their ear' do you have for Alex?"

Break state and review

24. Ask Alex to stand up and shake off observer position.

25. Review insights. What did Alex learn? Ask Alex to consider whether these points apply generally and not just to the specific relationship.

The subject ("Alex," in this case) need not vocalise every detail, as it's what happens inside that's important. You don't need to follow the instructions exactly, but maintaining the general form is essential. The detail will vary depending on what comes up—what the subject says. You must ensure, however, that the subject associates into each position (by accessing the VAK components) to intensify the insights they gain. You can use open questions to help them develop their understanding.

The following example is a transcript of this process in action.

From the example file

 The central figure here is someone I will call Karen ("K" below; I am "D"). Her grandson—let's call him John—was in her care. At age five, John was being disruptive at school, and the authorities were considering moving him to a special school—an outcome Karen didn't want. Karen had difficulty dealing with the professional care services involved, partly because they were focused on the boy, with little or no support to her, and perhaps because she was the grandmother rather than the mother.

D: Which of the people you have to deal with do you find most difficult?

K: The social worker.

D: What's the name of the social worker?

K: Mary Forsyth (Note: A fictional name has been substituted here.)

D: What would you call her?

K: Mary.

D: OK. I would like you to think of having a meeting with Mary here. Can you do that?

K: Yes.

D: Where will you sit?

K: Here.

D: Where will Mary sit?

K: There.

D: OK. Sit down in your chair, then.

K sits down in the chair she has chosen for herself. Her body looks tense.

D: So Mary is sitting over there. What does she look like?

K: She's short and a bit dumpy. Brown hair. She fidgets a lot.

D: How do you feel about Mary?

K: I feel she treats me like dirt on her shoe.

D: What do you actually feel?

K: I feel anxious.

D: Where is anxious in you?

K gestures to her upper body.

K: In my chest—a kind of tightness. Panic.

D: What do you say to yourself about Mary?

K: I wish she'd treat me with more respect.

D: So you'd like respect from her.

K: Yes.

D: OK. Stand up.

K stands up. D asks a question to help K shake off first position.

D: What's the time?

K: Half past ten.

D: OK. Come and sit over here.

K sits in the other chair. She seems more bunched up in this position.

D: OK. You're Mary now and Karen is sitting over there. What does Karen look like?

K as Mary: She's tall with long hair in a pony-tail. She's wearing jeans and casual shoes.

D: How do you feel about her?

K as Mary: I feel uneasy.

D: Where in you is that feeling of unease?

K as Mary: In my chest.

D: What kind of feeling?

K as Mary: Tightness.

D: Karen would like to have respect from you. What

behaviour from Karen would cause you, Mary, to treat Karen with respect?

K as Mary: More confidence.

D: So you would like Karen to be confident?

K as Mary: Yes.

D: OK. Stand up.

K stands up.

D: Come over here, please.

D and K walk some paces away.

D: So now you're an observer looking on—looking at Karen and Mary sitting talking. Can you see them?

K as observer: Yes.

D: If you could have a word in Karen's ear, what would you would you say to her?

K as observer: Be confident.

D: OK. Let's finish there.

D asks K a question to break state.

We also explored the relationship with her grandson and noticed some of his wants. I then showed Karen how to have feelings of confidence when she needed them by recalling times when things had gone really well. She also identified two significant things she could do to stimulate her grandson and displace some of his undesirable behaviour.

Some weeks later, the boy had settled down enough that the move to another school was no longer being considered. I can't say that the shifting chairs exercise made the difference, but it's possible that Karen changed enough to have had sufficient effect on John and on the professionals that the system of which they were all part moved to a new equilibrium, with the boy remaining at his existing school. That's how these things tend to work: little changes can make big differences in the wider system.

Now some years later, John is still in mainstream school and doing well. It turns out he has Asperger's Syndrome, a form of autism that affects social interaction.

Steps to take

- Work with a friend on the shifting chairs process, taking turns as the client and coach. Experience the effect and learn how the process works.

- Go through the exercise, either on your own or with someone else, taking as second position an inspirational person you would like to learn from but have never met.

- Run the exercise again, exploring the perspectives of family members. Try also taking the position of onlookers, friends possibly, who know your family well.

- If you are meeting someone for the first time and want the best possible result, use the process in advance of the meeting to review how you will come across.

- Before an important meeting on an issue with people you already know, use the technique to explore the perspectives of all the participants and investigate how you appear to each person.

Seeing ourselves in other people

We can learn about ourselves by noticing what we see in others. The opportunity to do this is around us all the time, and we can use it to great effect. We see in other people both attractive and unattractive aspects of ourselves. This is a consequence of a principle articulated by Carl Jung: we project behaviours we are not acknowledging about ourselves onto other people. When we notice another person's behaviour, especially when we have a strong emotional reaction to it, we will learn something if we ask ourselves, "How is that also my behaviour?"

In the family situation, projection can be particularly apparent because children often exhibit behaviour that is a close copy of their parent's behaviour. So when a parent sees behaviour they do not like in their child, it may well be a version of themselves they are noticing.

Projection is caused by part of our brain called the "reticular activation system," which filters the information we receive from our senses to reduce it to a manageable quantity. What we filter for is determined by the patterns we already have. An example of this effect is the situation I mentioned before: driving off in a new and, we think, unusual car and then noticing several of the same model. Our reticular activation system brings matching information to our attention. So it is with behaviour. If we notice someone's behaviour, it means we are noticing a matching pattern. "If you can spot it, you've got it," as they say. We have the structure of the experience. Conversely, we don't notice people doing things that are beyond our own knowledge.

In *Diamond Mind*, Rob Nairn said, "The average human mind tends to view its internal processes selectively. This means it sees only what it wants to see or is comfortable with. Everything else is repressed, denied, and projected."

We often discover symmetry in the shifting chairs exercise. When we go and sit in the other person's chair, we see the same issue with ourselves as we have projected onto them.

From the example file

📁 Helping mediate a commercial dispute, I was surprised at my own feeling of anger when one of the parties avoided taking responsibility for agreeing to a settlement by saying, "I will do it for my wife," thereby preserving his role as a victim. I realised later I was projecting my own avoidance of responsibility.

📁 I was struck by a friend's capacity to accept what had happened to her as a result of medical negligence and forgive the failings that led to her serious loss of physical capability. Reflecting on this later, I realised that my reaction meant that I had these capacities for acceptance and forgiveness, too, which was a profound learning for me.

📁 Jack believes Arthur to be untrustworthy, but it's not clear that his own behaviour is beyond reproach.

I imagine you may be sceptical about this projection effect, as I was at first. I suggest you put the scepticism to one side for a time and see what you learn about yourself and other people. "You'll see it when you believe it," not the other way around.

You can notice other people's projections. For example, several times I have watched complete strangers on a train discussing an absent third party with their travelling companion or on a mobile phone, criticising some behaviour, while simultaneously exhibiting that behaviour themselves.

The same effect is noticeable in disputes. Some people will be highly critical of others, accusing them, for example, of being arrogant and abusive, while simultaneously demonstrating their own arrogance and abusiveness. As Debbie Ford said in *The Dark Side of the Light Chasers*: "Our indignation over the behaviour of others is usually about an unresolved aspect of ourselves."

Steps to take

- Notice what you notice about other people, as well as your emotional response. Ask yourself: How is that also your behaviour?

- If you comment on others' behaviour, be aware you may be saying as much—or even more—about yourself as about the others.

- Observe other people and notice their comments about third parties. How is the behaviour they see in others also what you observe in them?

- Build a picture of yourself from what you notice about other people (your unconscious projections). In a group of people, you can get a sense of your overall make-up by adding up what you notice in all the other people present—a bit of this here, a bit of that there.

Seeing others as they see us

Just as we project unacknowledged aspects of ourselves onto other people and sometimes remark accordingly, other people project things onto us. So when they comment on our behaviour, we may realise that they are speaking about themselves as much as about us, without being aware they are doing that. Sometimes, it's much more their issue than ours.

Accepting ourselves

Typically, how we see ourselves, how we would like to see ourselves, and how others see us are all different. By bringing these three images closer together and ultimately merging them, we become much more real to other people—everything snaps into focus.

Our self-esteem depends on how well our self-image measures up to our ideal of ourselves. We can close the gap by either accepting what we can't change and so alter our ideal self to be realistic, or by improving our self-image by changing something about ourselves or by noticing qualities of which we may have been unaware, using the techniques we have discussed in this chapter.

By combining these approaches, we can make our self-image and our realistic ideal self the same. In other words, we can accept ourselves as we are.

We want to be sure that our self-image is an accurate reflection of how we come across to other people—that we have received and understood the feedback available from the "mirror" of people around us. If others sense that we have a good awareness of ourselves and that we are conscious of our choices of how to be, they are likely to stop expecting us to be something else—something we're not. Instead of several versions of ourselves seen by different people at different times, there's just one and everyone agrees what it is. With this clarity, we seem grounded and attractive to other people— three-dimensional. Once we accept ourselves, other people will accept us too. The effect is like murky water settling: suddenly everything is clear.

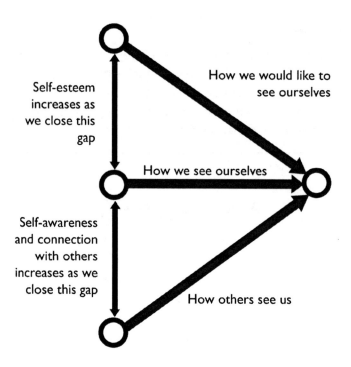

Self-esteem increases as we close this gap

How we would like to see ourselves

How we see ourselves

Self-awareness and connection with others increases as we close this gap

How others see us

Steps to take

🦶 What is there about yourself you might choose just to accept?

🦶 Where will your self-image, your ideal self, and others' images of you converge?

🦶 As an exercise and a bit of fun, consider this: if your self-image, your ideal self, and the version of you that others see were to meet, what would they say to each other?

🦶 Ask people who know you well what they most value about you or what you have done. The answers may pleasantly surprise you. Notice that they tend to project things about themselves onto you when they answer. They comment on their own attributes that they see in you.

🦶 As an exercise in self-esteem, divide your life to date into three equal periods of years and list your successes in each phase.

Step 9: Self-awareness

In summary

- The shifting chairs (perceptual positions) process helps us reflect on how we come across to other people and to make adjustments.

- We project onto other people things about ourselves, good and bad, as they do on us.

- Bringing our self-image, our ideal self, and others' images of us into line makes us seem fully real to other people, and they see clearly how to help us, perhaps for the first time.

Relating to you

- What have you still to accept about yourself?

- What will you do differently after reading this chapter?

Step 10:
Attention
to
yourself

Finding inner peace

Before	**After**
You may:	*You will:*
✗ Be unclear about what you want	✔ Move from problems to solutions
✗ Not communicate well to others how to interact with you or help you	✔ Be able to keep a solved problem solved
✗ Set goals for yourself that depend on others	✔ Have a process for developing "well-formed" outcomes
✗ Seek happiness only through material things and pleasurable pursuits	✔ Align your short-term actions with your bigger objectives
✗ Get stuck in problems	✔ Set goals that you can take full responsibility for
✗ Be unable to stop issues from recurring	✔ Understand the benefits of choosing your state and know that you can "step into" it
✗ Focus on what you don't want rather than what you do	✔ Be able to be at peace and still achieve what you want
✗ Be restless	✔ Have more success than you thought possible
✗ Waste the gift of life	✔ Make the most of the time you have

Step 10: Attention to yourself

Three things will help you be successful in your relationships with other people: Knowing what you want; letting go of whether you achieve that or not; and having the peace that comes from knowing you already have everything you truly need. As we will see, our focus is not so much what you want from other people as what you want for yourself in the context of your relationships—not quite the same thing.

Here, we look at an approach to developing and working on "well-formed" outcomes, building on what we covered in "Step 7: Values," and in particular, aligning our short-term actions and behaviours with what we want at a higher level. Ultimately, our "higher purpose" is a state of being rather than something we want to have or do, and so next we consider the benefit of simply choosing to be in that state. Finally, we discuss approaching our relationships with these things in mind.

First, though, we start with the importance of focusing on what we want rather than what we don't want.

Focusing on solutions

We can't solve our problems. We need to learn to outgrow them. Carl Jung

We are more likely to succeed by focusing on solutions rather than problems—on achieving what we do want rather than eliminating what we don't—because "energy flows where attention goes," or as Earl Nightingale said, "We become what we think about." Our attempts only to move away from a problem tend to fail in the long run, and we slip back into the difficulty. Wanting less of something will indeed cause us to move on, and may be the best motivation to get started, but it will not give us anywhere to go to. Without something to move toward, we get tired of keeping ourselves away from the problem and we fall back into it. A travel plan that only says, "Start here," won't take us very far.

In contrast, if we have a solution in mind, this gives us something specific to move toward. We have a destination, which, once attained, is a stable state. Viewed from the perspective of the solution, the problem typically looks a long way away and a long time in the past. We think, "I'm not going back there, not for anything." It's like climbing a hill: We may need to know what's on the other side before we have the energy to make the ascent in the first place, but once we're over it, we've moved on.

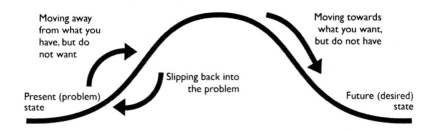

Moving away from what you have, but do not want

Moving towards what you want, but do not have

Slipping back into the problem

Present (problem) state

Future (desired) state

This is another perspective on one of the filtering patterns, Away from or Toward, which we covered in Step 5. It is better to filter for moving toward solutions rather than away from problems. Aiming to avoid something you don't want is like going shopping with a list of things that you don't need to buy. Even with the most disciplined Toward thinking, we'll still have enough Away from going on to detect trouble. If the problem is that important, it will break through our Toward preference and get our attention.

Say it the way you want it. Tad James and David Shephard

My own experience of the power of moving toward a solution rather than away from a problem happened in my marriage. When I got into a mess, a process of counselling was supportive, but I never really moved on, spending most of the time exploring the problems. I understood the issues better, but the best description of my progress would be that I went around in circles. About that time, I attended an introductory course in NLP. That was the turning point (and the beginning of the story of this book), and my life did begin to move forward. The critical difference was the solution focus—getting clear about what mattered in the future and moving toward that. Probably no marriage is perfect, and the flaws can seem much less important when we establish what really matters—our core values.

Focusing on what we want is very important. What we focus on grows, so if we dwell on anything other than what we want, we'll undermine our efforts to achieve it. The phrase "positive thinking" is often used, but I'm not sure that's completely helpful. "Positive" and "negative" imply a value judgment, which may differ from one person to another. It's better just to talk about what we want. We are also very susceptible to the fear of things going wrong, so we don't need to amplify difficulties much for them to become a dominant thought pattern, overwhelming our desire to move to a solution. Abraham Maslow said that high-achieving people take great care not to think about what they don't want.

 From the example file

Carol says she wants to have less stress. Until she focuses on moving toward something she wants instead, she's unlikely to eliminate stress from her life. With coaching, she realised she could aim for "calmness" rather than "less stress." This is much more likely to work.

Dropping the word "more" from what we want

In "Step 9: Self-awareness," we touched on the benefits of eliminating the word "more" from a goal. Instead of saying you want to "be more confident," say "be confident." The reason this matters is because "more confident" is an Away-from goal—away from the problem state of "less confident." "Be confident," on the other hand, is a Toward goal. If you set a goal to "be more confident," you can never finish. That way, there will always be more confidence to have or not have, and you will be vulnerable to being less confident and slipping right back to "not confident." Think of the hill again: "More confident" lies up the slope on the same side of the hill as "not confident." "Confident" is over the hill and down the other side. Once you're there, you've made it. Job done.

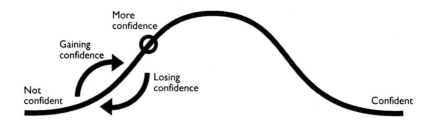

We can make the same point about being effective, organised, accepting, and many others.

Steps to take

 Think of a problem you have at the moment. How does your thinking change when you think of moving to a solution instead of trying to eliminate the problem?

 When you find yourself saying you want less of something, re-express your desire as a positive statement—something you want more of—then take the "more" way. How does that feel? Perhaps you are already at least halfway to what you want.

"Well-formed" outcomes

Now that we are focusing on what we want rather than what we don't want, we can look at a process for developing our desired outcomes. We can use this for everything from straightforward, everyday goals through to the highest levels of what we want to achieve in our lives. The sequence is as follows:

1. **State the outcome positively** in terms of something to move toward rather than away from—something concrete you want to happen.

2. **Set the context for achieving the outcome**—where, when, and with whom? The more specific the details the better because that will increase the likelihood of achieving the goal. Set actual dates, for example.

3. **Identify the higher purpose behind the outcome** and check that the two are aligned. What will achieving the outcome do for you? Is that what you want at the higher level? Perhaps the outcome you initially expressed isn't as well aligned as you thought, or maybe you can achieve the higher purpose in a better way.

4. **Establish the VAK** evidence for success by imagining you have already achieved the goal. What does that look, sound, and feel like? Describing the VAK elements of the outcome in the present tense greatly increases the likelihood of success because you are programming your unconscious to create the state you want and to recognise it when you experience it. You need to create your outcome in your head before you will be able to make it happen in reality.

5. **Keep the outcome "self-maintained"** so that achieving it doesn't depend on anyone else. You can then take full responsibility.

Dependence on the actions of others places your future in their hands, which is a primary cause of failure and stress. For example, to avoid this dependency, athletes set objectives based on achieving certain times rather than beating their competitors.

6. **Assess the cost of attaining your outcome** to determine whether it's worth it. It might not be. You incur a cost in doing one thing rather than another.

7. **Identify the "secondary gain"** that has sustained your present state, which serves you at some level—the benefit you get from staying where you are. This need won't go away of its own accord and must be met as the new outcome is achieved, or else challenged and re-evaluated. For example, a need for safety may stop you going to functions and events. To achieve an outcome of meeting new people, you need to find a way of being safe when you do go out.

8. **Identify the first step and commit yourself to powerful action.** Break the path to the outcome into small chunks. In the old saying, "if you have to eat an elephant, cut it into slices."

9. **Finally, check the "ecology" of what you are about to do** and make sure you mitigate the effects on other people. Who else may be affected?

The term "well-formed" implies an outcome that meets all the conditions within these steps. Once you have worked through this process, you only need to remember two things: "What's the outcome?" and "What's the next action?"

Take care not to set an emotional state such as "confidence" as an outcome to be achieved in the future because that needlessly delays having it. You can step into the desired state now, if you choose. (There is more on this below.)

The well-formed outcome process has a number of advantages over the more widely known "SMART" (Specific, Measurable, Agreed, Realistic or Relevant, Time-bound) objectives thinking.

• We are highly motivated to move to a solution that we have experienced in VAK terms (No. 4 in the well-formed outcome process) and with specific details about who else is involved, and where and when it takes place. We know how good we feel achieving the outcome. Our unconscious has experienced the desired state, knows how to recognise it, and is programmed to deliver or filter for what we want.

- We check that the outcome really will take us where we want to go (No. 3).

- With a self-maintained goal, we deliver our best without depending on other people (No. 5).

- We identify and resolve the secondary gain that keeps us where we are now. Without this step, we will not consistently or permanently achieve our outcome (No. 7).

- We resolve the implications for people around us (No. 9).

- We avoid limiting ourselves to "realistic" objectives, which can result in achieving below our potential. What "realistic" objective did Nelson Mandela set to free South Africa from apartheid, or Mahatma Gandhi to lead India to independence from British rule?

The greater danger for most of us lies not in setting our aim too high and falling short; but in setting our aim too low and achieving our mark. Michelangelo

Take great care not to limit your aspirations for yourself and for others. If you do have limits in your mind, you will not achieve beyond them. Maintain a belief that anything is possible. My wife and I take this principle very seriously indeed with our son who has autism. On the one hand, we accept that he may continue to have challenges, but on the other, we act as if anything and everything is possible in his development. The experience with autism has taught me just how important it is to remove any limits in our beliefs about what's possible in any aspect of our lives.

Our limitations tend to be conditioned in us, either by ourselves or by others. One place this happens is in the family. We tend to believe that it is wrong to succeed beyond the norms of the family; to do better than our parents, for example. Yet if we ask ourselves whether we as parents would want our children to do better than us, the answer most likely is "yes." So our parents will have thought that about us too. Yet many of us still live as their children, abiding by their values and beliefs, in effect seeking their approval, even when they are no longer around. To attend to ourselves, we may need to step out from our family's shadow, a frightening experience though that may be.

We sometimes hold on to beliefs in an attempt to show that we were right, but staying the same in order to justify how we were previously is especially limiting. To live life to the full, we need to accept that some of our beliefs may be outdated and replace them with ones that free us from unfounded limitations.

Understanding secondary gains can help us see why people stay the way they are when it seems to us that they would benefit from change. In extreme cases, they may continue a disagreement with someone because they benefit in some way. Perhaps that allows them to avoid confronting some issue of their own. Disputes sometimes continue just because the protagonists gain in some way from being in dispute. Bear this in mind before you commit to resolving an issue where this may be a factor.

The concept of a self-maintained outcome is very important in relationships. Being clear about the part of what we want that only depends on us helps us to make sure we achieve this. Success in relationships is not, in fact, a self-maintained outcome, whereas having an effective approach is. The only relationship for which we can have a self-maintained outcome is the one with ourselves. If we have a self-maintained outcome to perform well irrespective of what happens, we will do a better job and are more likely to achieve a useful result. Accept that what you want will come in time and be patient. The reward is calmness. In the old saying: "Infinite patience brings immediate results."

Steps to take

- Pick an outcome you want and develop it with the well-formed outcome process. You might want to do this with a friend coaching you. How does your thinking about the goal change? Expect to repeat the steps several times as you clarify your thoughts.

- If faced with a tedious or complicated task, visualise the job completed and notice how good it feels to have the end result. Explore the detail of the state. How exactly does it look? Now you will find your motivation to get the job done greatly increased (assuming the outcome is worthwhile).

- When you prepare for a meeting, consider carefully what your outcome should be. Make sure it is self-maintained. By all means, think about what you would like the other people to do, but set your desired outcome as something you can deliver that does not depend on them, such as making a presentation at the height of your capability. You'll find you get better results that way. Remember the story about athletes measuring themselves against the clock, not their competitors.

Aligning what we want with where we are going

In the process of developing "well-formed" outcomes, we align what we want with our higher purpose. We can think about our desires at two levels: the level of our specific outcome, or "first level" intention, and our "higher purpose"—where we are going. Achieving our first-level intention can sometimes fail to take us toward our higher purpose, because we don't realise at the start that our short-term actions won't take us where we want to go. Before we invest in any outcome, we can ask ourselves what achieving it will do for us and explore whether it is in fact the most appropriate goal.

We can choose how deeply we wish to explore the fit. We could do a simple check that a task will align with an overall plan or, at the other extreme, we could weigh whether a project really will give us the life we want. The further we take the process, the deeper the insights will be. We will need a chain of "What will that do for you?" questions to get to the ultimate higher purpose.

A sequence like this was a key moment for me. In a coaching session with a friend called Hazel, at a time when I was restless and driven, I talked about writing a book:

Hazel: So what's your outcome then?

David: To write a book.

Hazel: And what will that do for you?

David: I'll feel fulfilled.

Hazel: OK. And what will that do for you?

David: I'll be satisfied, I suppose.

Hazel: Yeah. And what will that do for you?

David: *Thinking, "What do you mean, 'what will that do for me?' My higher purpose is to feel fulfilled or satisfied."*
Feeling tense.
Pause...
With a big sigh and slumping shoulders,
Well, I suppose I'll be at peace then.

Hazel: Ah ha. So your higher purpose is to be at peace.

David: Er, yes. I suppose so.

Earlier, I had stopped at the higher purpose of "feeling fulfilled." Hazel pushed me further and helped me discover "being at peace" lay beyond "feeling fulfilled." (Years later, I now know that "peace" or something like it is what most people ultimately want deep down, although they might not know it yet.)

The "therapeutic" moment

This example illustrates the shift in "physiology" at the key moment of learning. When we discover something for ourselves, we typically change our breathing (with a sigh perhaps) and the position of our body, probably our shoulders. In coaching or therapy, this is called the "therapeutic moment" and signposts the importance of what we say, which may not be obvious just from the words. In relationships, if we miss similar signals coming from other people, we may lose opportunities to explore a key issue and move forward from that insight. None of us experience the same learning the same way a second time around, so the other person won't go through the same therapeutic moment even if the conversation were to be replayed word for word. So it's important to spot the physiological signals first time around.

A shift from "feeling fulfilled" to "being at peace" might seem like a small thing, but discovering that ultimately I wanted to be at peace and, in fact, could just choose that state (more on this below) was one of the most liberating things that has ever happened to me. My cultural background may have been making its presence felt here. In the "West of Scotland work ethic," life is about work, and if we're not struggling under a load, we're not living a good and "God-fearing" life. Now, I'm all for making the most of our time, but being driven like this may not be the best way to succeed.

Steps to take

- Consider something you believe you want. Ask yourself what achieving that will do for you. How well does the answer align with the big things you desire—your higher purpose? What changes might you make?

- When people say they want something and it's not clear to you what their purpose is, ask them: "What will that do for you?"

Sometimes, even as they answer, they'll realise their stated desire isn't the best approach to their bigger objective and modify what they say. At other times, you may help them see that they can achieve their goal a better way—or in a way that is more compatible with what other people want, and therefore, both more easily achieved and better aligned with the greater good.

 In your conversations, look out for the "therapeutic moment"— the sigh or movement that signals something has changed. What is the shift that you might have missed, were it not for the non-verbal signpost?

Choosing our state of being

Striving hard to achieve an objective or acquiring material things may not take us toward our higher purpose or help us attain a state that is good for our relationships. This flawed approach to achieving happiness, satisfaction, or inner peace involves the following sequence:

This approach doesn't work very well. No sooner have we completed an objective or acquired something and had a short spell of satisfaction, we want something more to feed the cycle. The harder we try to reach a state of happiness this way, the less likely we are to reach it. As Stephen Covey said, "Innocent pleasures in moderation can provide relaxation for the body and mind and can foster family and other relationships. But pleasure, per se, offers no deep, lasting satisfaction or sense of fulfilment."

We can break this cycle by adopting a different approach and choosing the state we desire and then "stepping into it," like this:

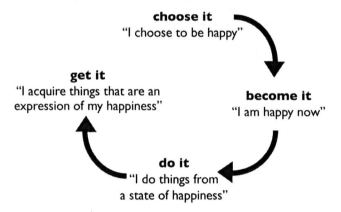

choose it
"I choose to be happy"

become it
"I am happy now"

do it
"I do things from
a state of happiness"

get it
"I acquire things that are an
expression of my happiness"

Just choosing to be in the state is easily said, but needs a little more explanation. The point is: We can choose our state, so it's better to do that first. Then we are much more likely to achieve the things we choose to do and enjoy the things we acquire. We could say that, in the first cycle, we are dominated by our ego, whereas in the second, we allow our "higher self" to take charge.

The way we feel—our state—is largely determined by what we think about and hold in our mind, and we can choose what that is. Our results in life tend to be determined by how we feel, so we should choose our thoughts carefully.

In the second Be—Do—Have sequence, the desired state could be our "higher purpose" that we explored in the "well-formed" outcomes process. Sometimes, we can just choose to be in the state and let go of the first level intention. We don't need it anymore. Or we adopt the desired state and stay committed to the outcome, but in the confidence that it fits with our higher purpose.

I can best illustrate the Be—Do—Have principle with my own example. As I recounted above, my friend Hazel helped me discover that my higher purpose was to be at peace, which seems so obvious now, but wasn't at the time. I struggled with this for a while: What's the meaning of life if we're not driven by a purpose? Maybe we're not meant to create our purpose. Perhaps it's inside. Searching long and hard in the world at large for a purpose in life might not work; whereas if we choose peace, our mission may come to us.

We detect rather than invent our missions in life. Victor Frankl

I must have read the Victor Frankl quote years ago, but not understood it. I had always put "achieving something in life" ahead of "being at peace," so I struggled to change that around. Accepting a life of being at peace, in which I may or may not achieve anything, was a challenge.

One of Carl Jung's principles is very helpful here: To not accept death is to not accept life. If we deny the prospect of death, we deny the prospect of life as well. If we live in fear of death, we squander the gift of life. If we accept the certainty of death, we can live life to the full in the meantime.

With the Be—Do—Have idea, my own way forward was obvious. Stop trying to do things (like write a book) to be fulfilled and instead just choose to be at peace. Just choose to be at peace. That's it. Let go. Accept everything. What's more, if I did write a book, it would be a better book. Who wants to read something written by someone who's driven and restless?

If we choose a resourceful state in this way, before setting off toward what we hope to achieve, we're less likely to be knocked off-course and are more likely to achieve our outcomes. That's the benefit of choosing and managing our state.

We can link all this with Wayne Dyer's teaching that our higher self just wants to be at peace. That's all it wants. The rest is our ego talking.

Sorting these things out is the true power and value and importance of NLP. Of course, there are other ways to the same ends, but none so quick that I know of. Hazel didn't realise what an impact she had made.

The question arises of how we maintain our chosen state. First of all, having once experienced it, we can get back to our desired state much more easily. We can repeat the process that got us there the first time. Specifically in the case of peacefulness, the techniques of peripheral vision and meditation we covered in "Step 3: Self-control" will greatly help.

Steps to take

What is the state of being you would like to have? What happens when you choose now to be in that state?

Outcome and higher purpose in relationships

All other things being equal, peacefulness helps your relationships. In fact, it's fantastically powerful. With the Be—Do—Have approach, we can choose our state independently of the people we are relating to, including our life partners. Before, we might have tried to do something like this:

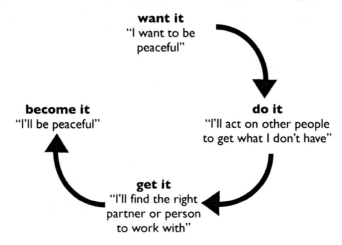

want it
"I want to be peaceful"

do it
"I'll act on other people to get what I don't have"

get it
"I'll find the right partner or person to work with"

become it
"I'll be peaceful"

We might act on our partners or the people we work with in order to arrive at a desired state ourselves, but our outcome is not self-maintained. We have made our state dependent on somebody else, which is not a good idea. Instead, we can break out of the trap by just choosing to be peaceful or whatever our desired state is. If "peaceful" isn't the right word for you, find the one that is—"at ease" or "happy" perhaps.

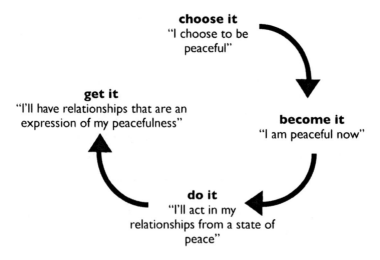

choose it
"I choose to be peaceful"

become it
"I am peaceful now"

do it
"I'll act in my relationships from a state of peace"

get it
"I'll have relationships that are an expression of my peacefulness"

Some of us feel we have no right to be happy when others are not, when there is so much suffering in the world; but unless we are happy, we are unable to give happiness to others.

If we're in a state of happiness or peacefulness, our partners, work colleagues, and friends are more likely to do things that support our state.

Can someone "make you happy?"

One of the most disempowering things that happens to us as we grow up is that parents and others encourage us to find partners that "make us happy." They are well meaning in that they intend to protect us from committing to unsuitable people, and it's obviously important that we team up with compatible partners. However, we end up with a belief that our happiness depends on someone else. It doesn't. A troubled relationship will tend to cause unhappiness, but doing something about that may be as much about choosing our state as it is about changing our partner.

Sometimes in relationships, if we can enlist the support of the other person, we can use the Be—Do—Have approach and just agree to choose to be in the state we want. That's partly what people who avoid getting bogged down in disputes do. They say, "We really don't want to be in a dispute, so how do we sort it out?"

Suppose we have a major argument with our partner (I know that's unlikely, but bear with me!). Saying, "We agree we want to stay together, so how do we resolve this problem?" puts a very different slant on the argument. It'll need to be resolved eventually, so why not now?

Turning to large-scale conflicts, the peace process in Northern Ireland shows that the sides in a dispute talk in the end. It might take many years, even decades before the circumstances can be made favourable, but the lesson is the same: eventually, the situation will be resolved or at least made tolerable through talking, so what's the point of waiting? Thinking of ongoing international conflicts: At some point in the future, the sides *will* have talked and come to a compromise. That will happen in the end, so how many years do we want to wait: 1, 10, 100? We could just do it now.

🦶 Asking about higher purpose helps resolve disputes. If you "chunk up" to the bigger picture enough times with "What will that do for you?"—you will find that both parties want the same thing: ultimately, to be at peace within themselves.

🦶 You can use this approach to chunk up your own intention to a level where you're confident that another person will have that desire too. Then you're in a position to say, "I believe we both want such and such, so here is my proposal...."

When you attend to yourself

When you focus on what you want rather than what you don't want, develop "well-formed" outcomes that align with your higher purpose and can be achieved without dependence on other people, and maintain a resourceful state, you will be effective in your relationships. Attention to yourself in this area gives you an inner peace and calmness that others find very appealing, reassuring, and powerful.

Sometimes, we may find it hard to be clear about what we want—we feel conflicted inside—but we can do something about that, and we look at how in "Step 11: Balance."

Step 10: Attention to yourself

In summary

- Focus on what you want instead of what you don't want.

- Use the well-formed outcomes process to develop your goals.

- Align your short-term actions with your higher purpose.

- Set objectives for which you can have full responsibility.

- Take great care to remove any limiting beliefs you have.

- Use the Be—Do—Have approach and take control of your state.

- Choose to be peaceful.

- Accept life.

Relating to you

- How will you attend to yourself in preparation for your relationships?

- What is the biggest learning you have taken from this chapter?

Step 11:
Balance

Getting into the groove

Before	After
You may:	**You will:**
✗ Be debilitated by inner conflict that you can't quite put your finger on or resolve	✔ Be familiar with your "parts" and how they make their presence felt
✗ Find yourself saying: "On the one hand, I would like...; on the other hand..." or "Part of me wants..." and similar phrases revealing inner tension	✔ Be able to resolve tension within yourself
✗ Seem unsure of yourself to other people	✔ Come across as congruent and balanced
✗ Have arguments with other people that are really about your own uncertainties	✔ Gain the energy and flow that come from being clear about what you want
✗ Be hard to help	✔ Resolve issues within yourself rather than playing them out with other people
	✔ Have a calming influence on others around you
	✔ Stimulate success in a group of people as they resolve conflict or accept their differences

Step 11: Balance

Of all the conflict we experience in our lives, sometimes the most debilitating is that which takes place within us. We can have a squabbling family of "parts" on the inside as much as a fractious group around us on the outside. Part of us thinks one thing; part of us thinks another. On the one hand, we have one view, but on the other hand, we have another. Should we do this or should we do that? Internal conflict often underlies our issues, and if it remains unresolved, we have little chance of being peaceful or of leading others. Each part sabotages the other's efforts to be successful.

Just as we can mediate between other people in our world, we can set up a negotiation between the various parts within ourselves and either integrate them into a whole or if that's a step too far, at least get them talking properly. Strangely perhaps, resolving conflict on the inside can be the most effective way to resolve issues on the outside, whether between ourselves and someone else or among other people. When we resolve tensions within ourselves, other people experience us as balanced, grounded, and real, and they are attracted to us. They tend to follow our lead.

Sometimes, we make other people play a role in what's really a debate within ourselves. We have an argument with someone where they take one side that really exists within ourselves. This is an aspect of projection—seeing ourselves in other people—that we covered in "Step 9: Self-awareness." Of course, we tend not to realise we're doing this at the time. Afterward, though, we can reflect on what happened and ask ourselves how we own the whole argument. Once we've resolved the issue within ourselves, we can go back and say to the other person, "I've been thinking about the issue and what I would like to propose is..." or something like that. In time, we will develop the presence of mind to notice ourselves projecting one half of our internal debate. We can then choose to resolve, or express, our own dilemma rather than let it come between us and other people.

Meeting the family within

We have a number of parts within us, almost like different people—not quite separate, though, as that would be a clinical condition. In healthy individuals, the different facets of our personality remain in communication with one another, although sometimes not very effectively. Some of our parts belong with the roles we have in our lives. In my case, examples would be father, husband, and engineer. We also have parts that relate to roles we had when we were younger, but that are apparently dormant now such as (for me): son, little boy, and student. Other parts may arise from needs we have, such as security, fun, and recognition.

We can benefit from thinking about what all our different parts may be and how they relate to each other. That's a task we're unlikely to finish, as aspects of ourselves may remain in our unconscious until something happens that causes them to make their presence known through inner tension around an issue we face. Then we have the real opportunity to identify the parts that are stirring up trouble, bring them out into the open, and find a way to negotiate a balance between them or merge them into a single part.

Balance on the inside

The first step in resolving inner conflict, after noticing it's happening in the first place, is to be clear about the parts of ourselves that are in tension with each other. The classic indicator is when we say, "On the one hand, I want one thing, and on the other, I want something else," or "Part of me..." or "Partly, I...." Getting into an argument with someone else would also tend to point to an inner conflict. What we do next is equivalent to the shifting chairs exercise in "Step 9: Self-awareness," where we moved between two chairs representing the position of the two people we wanted to focus on, one of them being ourselves. We could explore the two parts of ourselves by sitting first in one chair, then in the other (a technique used by Fritz Perls), but the more usual way is to take up the "on the one hand, on the other hand" pattern of speech and bring the parts out onto our hands, one per hand.

A coach would notice the language pattern, probably accompanied by hand gestures, and encourage the client to associate the two parts with their two hands. The client would end up holding both hands out in front, looking at them alternately and expressing the intentions, thoughts, and feelings of the part held in each hand. This might all sound bizarre, but it works. The use of the hands (or separate chairs) helps us to be clear about the different parts, which is a key step in resolving the conflict.

As we associate the parts with our hands, we can give a name or label to each. For example, I recently explored an issue around having the courage to be open. One part was my "leader" part and the other part was my "little boy" part.

We can form an image of the parts in our hands or close our eyes and imagine them there. We then communicate with each part in turn and ask it to establish what it sees, feels, and hears as it looks at the other part, thus deepening the experience. We then proceed to conduct a negotiation between the parts.

Here are the steps of the parts-integration process, from the beginning.

Steps to take

1. Describe the tension you are experiencing as, "On the one hand, I want _____, and on the other hand, I want _____."

2. Separate these two parts and associate one with each hand held out in front of you.

3. Describe the characteristics of each part and give them each a name or a label—some kind of identity, which could be a word or phrase such as "artist" and "provider," or "loving my work" and "need to pay the bills." Go for what fits for you. It doesn't matter whether it makes sense to anyone else.

4. Talk to one of the parts and establish what it sees, hears, and feels as it considers the other part. Invite the part to identify what it is about the other part that it is uncomfortable with.

5. Repeat step 4 for the other part.

6. Presupposing that each part has a positive intention toward the whole (you), what would those positive intentions be in each case? Communicate with each part and find out.

7. Notice that the parts do have a lot in common and that they could work together. (Seeking the higher purpose of each part's positive intention, or "chunking up," will eventually reveal that both parts have the same higher purpose—to be at peace or something similar.)

8. What gift (behaviour, belief, value, or "word in the ear") could each part offer the other? Ask the other part if it accepts the gift. At this point, you have established communication between the two parts and

increased their awareness of the other's point of view and intentions. That may be sufficient to resolve the tension and allow you to proceed.

9. You may wish to continue and integrate the two parts into one. Ask each part in turn whether it would be willing to pool its resources and integrate with the other. If both parts agree, then bring your hands together and pull them in toward your body, noticing how it feels to have these parts integrated together. What name would you give to the integrated part? Bring your hands all the way in to your body.

The key thing is that you explore the nature of the conflict between the parts and arrive at a settlement—at least an agreement to coexist in balance, accepting difference within you. Full integration may not be appropriate or essential. We're working here with aspects of our identity, so integration of our parts is like merging two of our roles into one—deciding that two things we do are actually two versions of the same thing. When we resolve the tensions, the common thread we end up with will be stronger than either part we started with.

An example of the kind of tension we are talking about is that on the one hand, we want success, but on the other, we want safety. Making the most of our talents seems to involve placing ourselves at risk. The result can be that we sabotage ourselves to avoid being at the centre of attention for too long. Just when we get ourselves in a leading position, we are shocked at our own power reflected back from other people, and we do something quickly to deflect it away, thus spoiling our own performance.

I explored this issue recently as a parts problem I had, where my "leader" part, whose positive intention toward me was to be all I could be and make the most of my life, and my "little boy" part, whose positive intention was to keep me safe. In this case, I found the leader could learn from the little boy, who wanted the leader to know that there is safety in vulnerability, as opposed to layers of protection, because other people respond well to openness and honesty and distrust those who pretend to be something they're not. The following day, somebody remarked that by choosing to be vulnerable, the leader in me was truly leading.

Steps to take

 Think about an issue where you feel conflicted between alternative courses of action. What are the parts of you that give rise to this tension? Work through the parts integration process and see what way forward comes to you. Often, the new alternative will be more than the sum of the two original choices with the qualities of each combined in some way. You could have a friend coach you through the process.

We frequently make the mistake of expecting other people to be completely consistent in their decisions and actions when, in reality, they probably struggle with internal conflict just as much as we do, or more. It's strange to expect other people to be integrated, when we know how difficult it is to be that way ourselves. If they have conflict within and treat themselves with distaste, then they will treat us the same way, just as we would treat them if the roles were reversed.

From the example file

 Alice seems to have low self-esteem. She treats herself without love or respect and behaves the same way toward others, whose reactions to her behaviour just tend to reinforce her pattern. She seems to be conflicted about the job that she does and perhaps would rather be doing something else. For her self-esteem and behaviour to improve, she needs to resolve her inner conflict, either by changing her job or by recognising that her current role fits more fully with her needs than she sometimes feels.

Steps to take

 Consider the people around you who seem to behave inconsistently. How does your impression of them change if you recognise that they may have unresolved conflict within themselves—parts that have not accepted each other? What will you do differently in the light of seeing them this way?

Notice the symmetry between the parts-integration process and the shifting chairs (Perceptual Positions) exercise we covered in "Step 9: Self-awareness." They are two versions of the same thing. The shifting chairs process works because conflict with other people tends to be an expression of tension within ourselves that we're not recognising, but which we can draw out by moving from one chair to the other and "sitting" in our projections. There is a parallel here: If our environment is cluttered, our mind tends to be cluttered. If we want more focus in our heads, tidying up our home or our desk is a good way to start. So: cluttered on the outside, cluttered on the inside; conflicted on the outside, conflicted on the inside. Or orderly on the outside, orderly on the inside.

Balance on the outside

Once we have balance within ourselves, we are available to promote balance in the world around us. Balance is the key to moving forward—balance within ourselves, balance between ourselves and others, and balance between other people.

Some apparently believe a "win–lose" outcome in their favour can be good for them, but I've never seen "win–lose" turn into anything other than "lose–lose." It might take years, but lose–lose is the outcome in the end. Win–lose is not the way to inner peace. On a number of occasions, I have won something at someone else's expense and regretted it later. I lost more than I gained.

A "win–lose" mentality can wreak havoc in any domain of human life.
William Ury

Stephen Covey wrote, "Anything less than Win/Win in an interdependent reality is a poor second best that will have impact in the long-term relationship. If you can't reach a true Win/Win, you're very often better off to go for No Deal."

With other people, imbalance will arise from values that are in conflict. In that sense, conflict is ever-present. Just recognising that and knowing what the conflicted values are is a useful step. We then have the option of accepting the differences and finding a point of compromise with a net gain for both. Often, people will accept another's intentions once they know what their values are.

Getting into the groove

To move quickly and well, we need balance, and that's true both within ourselves and with other people. We don't necessarily need to have the same values or precisely the same intentions, but we need to have a purpose in common, a shared interest in an outcome.

We can think of many analogies. The one that is most familiar to me is that of a sailing vessel. Without the sails being set just right and correctly balanced with the helm and the trim of the boat, the yacht won't be "in the groove" and won't sail at her best. Similarly, a tightrope-walker won't get very far without balance, neither will a golfer or a tennis player or any other sportsperson. I believe that organisations do best when they are at the point of balance as well—and families too, for that matter. Some debate and discussion is healthy, but eventually, everybody needs to put themselves on the same side; otherwise, the tension will be destructive. We're looking for the "sweet spot" or the "zone" where there is a balance between the objectives of the participants. If we find it, the results can be many times better than if we continue with unresolved tension.

Achieving balance or congruence within ourselves also applies to much of what we have covered already. We want a balance:

• Between attention to others and attention to ourselves

• Between VAK channels

• Between extremes of filtering patterns

• In self-control through calmness

• Within our own values

• Through fair and precise language

• Among first-, second-, and third-position perspectives

Richard Bandler and John Grinder wrote: "Other people's experience of a congruent human being is usually described in terms of that person's having personal presence, knowing what he is talking about, being charismatic, dynamic, and a host of other superlatives."

We turn in the final Step to the one remaining ingredient that helps make all this possible: love.

Step 11: Balance

In summary

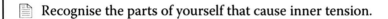 Recognise the parts of yourself that cause inner tension.

Use the parts-integration process to negotiate an internal agreement.

When you find yourself in an argument, reflect on how that may be an outward expression of an inner conflict and work on it accordingly.

Be alive to the possible consequences of inner conflict in other people.

Promote balance around you through the influence of your congruence and find the equilibrium from which results can flow.

Relating to you

What will balance bring to your life?

What are you going to do differently after reading this chapter?

Step 12:
Love

Going beyond yourself

Before *You may:*	After *You will:*
✗ Approach relationships only in a rational way	✔ Be comfortable with the emotional dimension
✗ Think that if we can't prove something, it can't be right	✔ Be open to the possibility that some things work even though we can't explain them
✗ Want evidence for everything	✔ Choose to displace fear in yourself and in other people
✗ Disregard the possibility that there may be some things that we just can't quite explain	✔ Speak from the heart
✗ Act out of fear	✔ Keep a spiritual perspective in mind
✗ Have a rather empty experience of life	✔ Act out of love
	✔ Live an enriching life

Step 12: Love

*I may be able to speak the languages of men and even of angels, but if
I have no love, my speech is no more than a noisy gong or a clanging bell.*
I Corinthians 13

When I set out to write this book, I never dreamt I would add a chapter on love—I'm an engineer, for goodness sake. Yet the more I worked on the rest of the material, the more I found that a systematic approach to relationships only seems whole with love and a sense of spirit included.

What do I mean by love? I am going to borrow M. Scott Peck's definition from *The Road Less Traveled*: "The will to extend one's self for the purpose of nurturing one's own or another's spiritual growth." Scott Peck also wrote: "Since it requires the extension of ourselves, love is always either work or courage. If an act is not one of work or courage, then it is not an act of love. There are no exceptions."

M. Scott Peck discounts the notion of "romantic love," and I am not going to address the subject of attraction between partners either, other than to say that the skills in this book can greatly help you if that's your present priority. Rather, I am going to restrict my comments to the love defined by M. Scott Peck and referred to in the Corinthians passage.

Looking over the books I have read either by or about those men and women who led the way in helping others unblock their lives and their relationships, I am struck by how their love for the people they worked with radiates from the pages. I connect all of that with something much closer to home for me:

From the example file

 My father was a leading surgeon and taught many younger medical professionals over the years. From time to time, I still meet a few of them, now in the later stages of their careers or retired. One (who continues to hold high office) told me that he learned many things from my father, lots of them about medicine, of course. But above all, he said, he learned how to "be nice to people," getting "where he is today" by acting on those lessons. My father has been dead for nearly 30 years, but on meeting his younger colleagues, their love for their teacher and his love for them come across so strongly that I am almost overwhelmed.

Only recently did I notice how the sources for this book and these memories of my father are connected by love.

We might question whether love (and being nice to people) has any place in the cut-and-thrust world of business and other organisations, where ruthless competition, job losses, and management of performance may be the dominant themes. Some would say that in business, being nice to people and profitable results are mutually exclusive. I don't think so. Even in fulfilling our responsibilities to shareholders, even at the extreme of terminating an employee's contract, for example, we can act compassionately, even though the message is a hard one.

I am not suggesting being soft as a manager. In management roles, we have a duty to be firm but fair—to administer "tough love," if you like.

In *Good to Great*, Jim Collins said, "Members of the good-to-great teams tended to become and remain friends for life." He continued, "The people we interviewed from the good-to-great companies clearly loved what they did, largely because they loved who they did it with." Some businesspeople I know will only work with people they like. They probably wouldn't dare say it, for fear of being misunderstood, but I believe they are expressing the desire for love to flow around the relationship and the work. If our working lives don't result in lasting friendships, it seems to me that we're not approaching them effectively, and our results will suffer accordingly.

Genuine love respects people as individuals and seeks to help them develop and grow in their own right. This is so in the workplace and particularly important in the context of marriage and other intimate relationships. As M. Scott Peck said, "It is at the moment when the mating instinct has run its course that the opportunity for genuine love begins."

It is often said that "love" is a verb. I have found this a helpful thought. In the busy-ness of life, we can find opportunities to love in the most mundane of things. For example, most nights I wash the dishes. I can regard that as a chore to be done or an opportunity to do something in a loving way, by doing that little bit more than the job requires. The tasks have to be done anyway, so I might as well make the best of the time involved. It's surprising what a difference that makes.

We must also recognise what love is not. In the marital relationship, love does not mean never doing anything without the other partner. It does not mean always doing what the other partner says or giving them what they want or knowing what they want before they ask. None of these equate to love. None of them fit with the definition from *The Road Less Traveled*.

My suggestion is that you regard love as something you do rather than something you have, whatever the context. Keep M. Scott Peck's kind of love in mind as you relate to other people.

Overcoming fear with love

You can assume virtually everyone you meet or know lives in a state of fear. Only the intensity of it varies. Eckhart Tolle

Ultimately, we only have two fundamental emotions—fear and love. Fear arises from the ego, which wants us to be separate from other people. Love stems from the higher self, which just wants to be at peace. We can boil everything down to one principle: acting from love instead of from fear. If we act in a way that drains our energy, we are acting from fear. If we act from love, our energy grows.

If you notice yourself acting from fear, stop. What if you were to act from love, what would you do then? If we choose to act with an inner sense of love or compassion, we transcend fear, with benefits for our organisations and ourselves. If you doubt that, think of the individuals who are a byword for compassion, such as Mahatma Gandhi, Mother Teresa, and Nelson Mandela.

This principle of acting from love rather than fear is an ancient philosophy. The appropriateness in the home or family environment is plain, but perhaps it's less obvious in the work environment. Yet our organisations are full of people acting out of fear. In "Step 7: Values," we talked about the unmet need for security, which is a major factor in our lives. People and organisations around us are predominantly acting out of fear. As Parker J. Palmer said, "Fear is everywhere—in our culture, in our institutions, in ourselves—and it cuts us off from everything." Think back to Maslow's Hierarchy of Needs: Security needs are second from bottom in the hierarchy, so if most people have unmet needs at that level, they're not going to be very productive, and the same, therefore, goes for our organisations. We're too busy being fearful to think at our best.

As human beings, we seem predisposed to fear, which is why focusing on what we want rather than what we don't want is so important. We can lead ourselves and others away from fear, however, by acting out of love and, in so doing, achieve great things.

Trust and openness

We all know that people who trust each other can be very productive and achieve exceptional results even with poor resources, whereas even if they are provided with the latest equipment and lots of money, people who don't trust each other will still fall well short of targets that might be set. We know this to be true, and yet in our organisations, we tend to persist in acting as if emotional connections have nothing to do with results and the "bottom line."

We will have the greatest connection with people if we act from our heart, with all the truthfulness we can muster. That openness requires trust. Be aware of the trust others have in you and be careful to honor and nurture it, by respecting confidences, among other things. Take care with the trust you place in others.

Being prepared to accept the unexplained

Love is hard to understand and explain, or perhaps it's easy if we open our minds a little. Many of us have been taught to seek evidence or a scientific explanation before committing to anything. (That goes for me as an engineer more than most.) Unfortunately, that training sets up a limiting belief that if we can't explain something or don't have evidence, it can't be right. The field of science is littered with examples of beliefs now held to be true that, at one time, people were ridiculed or worse for proposing. Classic examples are the earth being spherical rather than flat and orbiting the sun instead of the other way round.

Any time you feel absolutely certain of something, that's a sure sign that you have missed something. Richard Bandler

So it is with people and relationships. Things happen that we can't explain. Keep an open mind about what's going on. With some things, "we see it when we believe it," not the other way around. Public policy perhaps should be based on evidence, but as individuals, we can be free of that constraint and recognise that there is more to life than that which we can physically prove.

A sense of spirit

Contemplating our approach to relationships for any length of time leads us to think about both what we're really here in this life to do and what happens when we're gone. Some sense of a personal answer to these questions helps us relate to other people, not to foist beliefs on them, but because a person with a sense of faith has a reassuring presence. The one thing we all have in common, apart from paying taxes (which isn't really the same for all of us), is that someday we aren't going to be around anymore. What happens then? Other people are looking for answers to that question just as much as we are.

Until recently, alluding to a spiritual perspective would have seemed to me a walk into the unknown, but I've come to regard it as a shortcut to relationships and something that completes the picture of everything else we have covered. Having studied something of what goes on between human beings in their relationships, my sense is that there is more going on than we can explain at the physical level. Albert Einstein seemed to have had this view when he wrote: "I am not interested in this spectrum of light, or how much this molecule weighs, or what this particular atomic structure is. I want to know God's thoughts. Everything else is details." He also said: "God shows himself in a harmony of everything that exists," which we might relate to the subject we covered in "Step 11: Balance."

I mention all this, not to push a religious message (I don't have one), but to tell you that working on a systematic way of relating to other people and much examining of the practical details has taken me, not further away from a spiritual understanding, as you might have expected, but closer to one. There's something about the simplicity and "groundedness" of NLP and the other ideas we have covered that opens the door to a faith in something eternal. Eckhart Tolle wrote: "In essence, there is and always has been only one spiritual teaching, although it comes in many forms. Some of these forms, such as the ancient religions, have become so overlaid with extraneous matter that their spiritual essence has become almost completely obscured by it."

Both Parker J. Palmer and Stephen Covey emphasise the interdependence of faith, emotion, and logic. Parker J. Palmer wrote: "Intellect, emotion, and spirit depend on one another for wholeness." Stephen Covey talked of the ancient Greek philosophy combining ethos, pathos, and logos, meaning your character (or the faith people have in your integrity and competency), emotion (your relationships), and logic (your reasoning).

Keep in mind the possibility of a spiritual dimension because it may be that you need to recognise one to excel in your relationships. Sometimes, taking a spiritual perspective is the quickest way to solve the apparently mundane.

When you act out of love

If love is not enough, neither is punishment; the two together can be remarkably effective in changing behaviour. Frank Farrelly and Jeff Brandsma

All we have covered in this book is diminished if we have no love. I have mentioned the importance of using the skills in this book with integrity. I could equally have said with love, which transcends everything we have covered so far. Love is not a finite commodity. Unlike many things, the more you give, the more you have.

The majority of people you meet won't have the skills we have covered in this book. Accept that the quality of your actions may not be matched by others, at least not at first—this is all the more reason to continue. Some may even react against you because your balance and love challenges their patterns and confronts them with their own issues. If you meet people who gain in some way from conflict, you will be a threat to them, but love is more powerful than anything they have.

If you don't love humanity, you're on the wrong planet. Jay Abraham

Steps to take

- Bring a sense of love into what you do.

- Be sensitive to the emotional state of the people you relate to and treat that as something you might be able to influence. Unmet needs drive emotions, so think what's missing and act accordingly.

- Keep in mind the span of a life and what really matters.

- Be open to the spiritual perspective in your relationships.

- Remember the Buddhist principle: Be compassionate toward those less enlightened than yourself.

Too few of us are capable of employing power with love. More of us need to learn. Adam Kahane

Step 12: Love

In summary

- Displace fear with love, both in yourself and in other people.

- Be prepared to accept the unexplained.

- Embrace openness.

- Nurture trust.

- Be open to the spiritual dimension in your relationships, whatever that means for you.

- Be compassionate toward others.

Relating to you

- How will you allow love to enrich your life?

- What's different for you now after reading this chapter?

Applying
the
Steps

Being effective now

Before *You may:*	After *You will:*
✗ Wonder how best to apply the Steps to specific situations	✔ Be clear about which skills are most important in specific applications
✗ Fail to make the most of what you have learned	✔ Make the most of your learning
✗ Miss opportunities to improve your relationships and your life	✔ Be able to apply the Steps to other areas of your life
✗ Allow problems to build up unnecessarily	✔ Know where to start when new issues arise
✗ Be unable to resolve disputes and disagreements	✔ Have many more options for avoiding disputes and resolving them if they happen
	✔ Tackle issues you have now and make a difference straight away

Applying the Steps

We have completed our path through the 12 Steps and experienced them as both a journey and as a powerful system for getting along with the people we need to get along with. In this chapter, we look at applying the Steps in a number of contexts, noting the skills that are most relevant in each case.

Exactly how you blend the Steps with your other capabilities is an individual matter. My presentation of them is no doubt coloured by how I interpret my roles such as husband, father, company director, engineer, project manager, consultant, and friend. You may not agree with what I say—so much the better if you have your own ideas. Although much will apply directly, you will have areas of your life where you will need to work out how to apply the Steps for yourself.

Here, we look at some specific applications under five headings:

Starting out
• Establishing relationships quickly and reliably
• Engaging others confidently and with inner confidence
• Getting what you want by helping others get what they want

Leadership
• Getting people to work together
• Gathering support for a common goal
• Exercising power with integrity
• Leading with authority and compassion

Conflict
• Sorting out personality clashes
• Accommodating differences
• Resolving disputes
• Dealing with difficult people

Commerce
• Selling
• Managing relationships where money is involved

Family
• Succeeding with partners
• Parenting

Of course, all the Steps apply to a degree in every situation, and the table and the sections that follow indicate only which are the most important in each case. In life, we only have so much time and attention, so we need to choose where to apply our learning effort. This chapter will help you prioritise.

Application (Steps)	1: Attention to others	2: Attitude	3: Self-control	4: Wavelength	5: Filters	6: Connection	7: Values	8: Language	9: Self-awareness	10: Attention to yourself	11: Balance	12: Love
Establishing relationships quickly and reliably	✓	✓		✓	✓	✓	✓		✓			
Engaging others confidently and with inner confidence	✓	✓	✓	✓	✓	✓	✓		✓			
Getting what you want by helping others get what they want	✓	✓		✓		✓	✓		✓			
Getting people to work together	✓	✓					✓		✓		✓	
Gathering support for a common goal	✓	✓					✓					
Exercising power with integrity	✓	✓	✓				✓				✓	
Leading with authority and compassion	✓	✓	✓			✓	✓		✓	✓	✓	✓
Sorting out personality clashes and other accidents		✓	✓	✓	✓	✓		✓	✓			
Accommodating differences		✓	✓	✓	✓	✓	✓		✓			
Resolving disputes		✓	✓	✓	✓	✓	✓	✓	✓		✓	✓
Dealing with difficult people	✓	✓	✓			✓	✓	✓	✓	✓		
Selling	✓	✓		✓	✓	✓	✓		✓			
Managing relationships where money is involved		✓					✓			✓	✓	
Succeeding with partners	✓	✓	✓				✓	✓	✓	✓	✓	✓
Parenting	✓	✓	✓				✓	✓			✓	✓

Placing the entries in this table is a subjective process, and you might well tick other boxes and come up with a different picture. Counting the number of times the Steps are highlighted, the top five are:

Step 2: Attitude

Step 7: Values

Step 1: Attention to others

Step 9: Self-awareness

Step 3: Self-control

This list suggests that if we manage our attitude by living the NLP presuppositions, pay attention to values, focus on other people, and have a high level of self-awareness and self-control, we'll do pretty well (at least if we're acting out of love rather than fear).

Counting across the rows, the most demanding situations are:

• Resolving disputes

• Succeeding with partners

• Leading with authority and compassion

• Dealing with difficult people

• Engaging others confidently and with inner confidence

These are the areas where the skills may make the most difference. These two lists do seem to reflect what we might superficially expect.

In the sections that follow, we'll cover some details on how the Steps apply to each situation. As we do, we'll pick up some points about the NLP presuppositions we covered in "Step 2: Attitude." Adopting a resourceful attitude and frame of mind is a vital beginning in every application.

References to the Steps are indicated by the numbers in parentheses. A list of the Steps is included in the summary at the end of the chapter.

Starting out

Establishing relationships quickly and reliably

When we first meet someone, we may not have very long to connect with them. The most reliable approach is to focus on the other person initially (1) and find out what is important to them (7), while paying attention to building rapport (6). We may need to say a little about ourselves first and should be prepared to do that. Indeed, we may meet people who apply the same approach to us, in which case we should go along with their wishes and talk about ourselves. We will be attending to them by letting them control the conversation.

We can tune in to the other person's Wavelength (4) and Filters (5) and use this knowledge to adjust what we say and what we ask. Well-developed Self-awareness (9) will help us come across well.

Steps to take

- Everybody understands the world differently. Respect that.

- Take responsibility for the effect of what you say if the reaction isn't what you expect.

- If the person you have just met does or says something you find hard to accept, consider the underlying intention.

- As a conversation unfolds, aim to move fairly quickly to what matters to the other person. Look for values you have in common. How do the possibilities open up as you discover what the other person finds important?

- If you see little opportunity for mutual benefit, you could respectfully say that it has been a pleasure to meet and politely move on.

Take your time forming an impression of someone. As the NLP presupposition says:

The identity of a person is different from the behaviour they demonstrate.

Engaging others confidently and with inner confidence

What do we mean by confidence? My dictionary gives various definitions, among them:

firm trust or belief, faith, self-reliance, firmness, boldness, presumption

There is both an inner side and outward side to confidence. On the one hand, we may act in a manner that others would perceive as reflecting the definition, and on the other, we may or may not feel assured inside ourselves when we do so.

Is confidence always welcomed? When does confidence become arrogance? This may be a familiar but unresolved conundrum. We can label "confidence" and "arrogance" when we see them, but how do we ensure that we come across as confident rather than arrogant? Engaging others confidently and with inner confidence is the outcome we achieve when we deploy the skills we have learned: Attention to others (1), Self-control (3), and Self-awareness (9), as well as the rapport-building (6) and tuning-in aspects (4, 5). An awareness of values (7) will also help us. Working with these Steps will ensure we are confident in a pleasant and acceptable way.

Other people can be confident without being arrogant, so we can too:

If it's possible in the world then it's possible for me, if only
I can discover the "how."

Getting what you want by helping other people get what they want

How do we go about getting what we want? I used to believe that the best way is to state our case as powerfully as we can. This may work some of the time, but the bigger and more important the goal, the less likely we are to succeed with this method. Even if a strong argument does work, we may use up some or all of the goodwill in the relationship. We need another approach, preferably one that increases, rather than diminishes, the connection and achieves balance and a "win–win" result.

A better approach is to discover what matters to the other person (1, 7), paying attention to that first, and then figure out how their need can be met along with our own objective. Human nature is such that if we help other people, they will tend to help us. We want to be clear about our own outcome (10) beforehand. Filtering patterns (5) may be relevant, especially if the other person has an Away-from orientation. Their use of language (8) may give us openings to move toward mutual benefit. Remember:

The person with the greatest flexibility of thinking and behaviour is likely to have the greatest influence.

Steps to take

 Find the flexibility to help the other person get what they want as you achieve what you want.

Leadership

Getting people to work together

Find out what's important to all the individuals (1, 7) and show them how they have more to gain by working together rather than separately. Look for the balance in the situation (11). Where is the "sweet spot" through which results can flow? Focus on what you want to happen because:

Energy flows where attention goes.

Awareness of how you come across (9) will help you be effective in leading other people.

Steps to take

 Respect everybody's values, beliefs, and models of the world.

 Ensure everybody feels involved and consulted.

Gathering support for a common goal

Getting people to support a shared objective involves paying attention to them (1), finding out what they want (7), and organising things so that all the players get at least some of what they want by supporting the common goal. The key is values—finding out what matters. Several of the NLP presuppositions merit a comment here:

The map is not the territory	The stakeholders all have different models. Part of the process of gathering support involves developing their "maps" so that they see how the common goal fits with their objectives.
The person with the greatest flexibility of thinking and behaviour is likely to have the greatest influence.	That needs to be you.
People have all the resources they need to make whatever changes they choose.	They can support the proposal if they like. Find out how they want to.
There is no such thing as failure, only feedback.	If you don't get agreement at first, that's feedback that you haven't made the right proposal yet.
There is a solution to every problem.	There is a deal to be done.
Energy flows where attention goes.	Emphasise the things that unite the people involved.

Of course, this assumes that individual values are sufficiently aligned that common cause is possible. If that's not the case, making the reality visible and deciding what to do about it will bring the time-wasting to an end. It's better to decide that a common goal isn't achievable and move on with something else than continue to invest time and energy in a doomed effort.

Exercising power with integrity

Even if we have power as a result of our position, we will get the best results if we use it sparingly and save it for when we really need it. The rest of the time, common courtesy works perfectly well and is a better option. Invest in the relationships when you have the time so that you can rely on them when you don't. Thinking about things from others' points of view (1)—and what will work for them or what's important to them (7)—will help you achieve the results you want. Self-control (3) and an inner balance (11) will help you use your power appropriately ... and increase it, too.

Leading with authority and compassion

The difference between this topic and the previous one is in the degree to which you transcend the everyday and mundane by connecting with people (6) at a deep, profound, and inspiring level by appealing to what matters to them (7) and conveying a sense of being involved in something bigger and longer-lasting than ourselves (12). The more Self-control (3), Self-awareness (9), and Balance (11) you have—and the clearer you can be about attending both to others (1) and to yourself (10)—the better you will be able to do this.

Conflict

Sorting out personality clashes and other accidents

Sometimes, we perceive a mismatch between two people or between ourselves and somebody else—what we might call a "personality clash." Something keeps cropping up in the relationship and stopping useful things happening. We tend to talk about a personality clash as if we can do nothing about it, but we can understand the causes, avoid victim language, and do something to improve compatibility.

Mismatches in what people want are obvious enough, but we are talking about something more subtle here. Many so-called "personality clashes" result from mismatches in VAK preferences (4), filtering patterns (5), or body language (6), and because all these aspects are largely unconscious, we're not aware of the incompatibility. Using our skills in these areas, we can look for the cause and decide what to do differently to avoid the difficulty. Self-control (3) will help us, as will Self-awareness (9). Language patterns (8) may also reveal issues that we can work with. Just because two people are mismatched in some ways doesn't mean that they are incompatible. There is a way to resolve a mismatch. We just need to find it.

Accommodating differences

We are all different to a greater or lesser degree, and conflicted aspirations are ever-present. Accepting that and respecting difference is liberating when we stop trying to make the world fit in with us. Differences are also an opportunity to learn.

Our models of the world are not the same, and we operate in accordance with different values and beliefs. The world is a diverse place. We value different things, but nothing is objectively right or wrong. People make choices in accordance with their model of the world. That's all any of us can do.

Different values will drive behaviour that sometimes clashes with ours, but that clash is probably not deliberate. The other person has just as much right to their values as we have to ours.

Accepting difference can be easier if we find what we have in common. More unites us than divides us. If nothing else, most of us want to feel good, have some fun from time to time, and make the most of our lives. Values (7) are a short-hand for understanding the differences that are at work and identifying ways to deal with them or accommodate them. We may be able to relate at a higher level than the level at which the problem appears. If we are in difficulty at the behaviour level, we will find something in common at the values level if we look hard enough.

Being as well tuned to the other person as possible (4, 5) will help us deal with differences, as will Self-control (3) and Self-awareness (9). If we work hard at building rapport (6), the investment in the relationship will help to carry it through the difficult times that come about due to the differences between us.

Resolving disputes

The only safe way to destroy your enemy is to make him your friend.
Abraham Lincoln

When conflicted values and mismatched personalities cause actual disputes, we need to move beyond accommodating differences and apply stronger medicine. In the full-blown form, we are then into the twin territories of negotiation and mediation, which are beyond the scope of this book. (William Ury and Ken Cloke's works are a good place to start.)

The Steps we have covered here may well be sufficient to resolve disputes at an early stage and, perhaps more importantly, may well help stop conflict from developing into actual dispute. Start with Self-control (3). Finding compatible communication styles (4, 5), managing rapport as a resource (6), and working with language patterns are all going to help, as will understanding the Values (7) in play. The shifting chairs technique (9) is a useful method of getting one side to see another side's point of view and also to see how their approach looks from an objective viewpoint. The Language (8) that people use in a dispute provides fertile ground for intervention. Your own Balance (11) will be influential, as will a sense of faith, hope, and indeed, Love (12).

My experience of disputes that go as far as litigation and the courts is that shortcomings in relationship skills are usually a factor somewhere. That's good news because it means with a bit more skill, we can have fewer disputes and more easily resolve the ones that do occur.

In *The Third Side*, William Ury talks of the important contribution that can be made by those close to the participants in a dispute—"the third side." All of the Steps are good tools for a "third-sider." Ken Cloke (*Mediating Dangerously*) suggests that the role of mediator is to be "on everybody's side."

Sorting out disputes can be sufficiently challenging that all the presuppositions have their relevance:

The map is not the territory	Many things can be simultaneously valid and coexist together—much more than we commonly allow for. Observing disputes, I am struck by how one side will assert one thing and then the other side will assert another as if the two statements were mutually exclusive, when often they can easily both be true at the same time.
The meaning of any communication is indicated by the response it gets.	Have each side take responsibility for the effect of its communication.
Mind and body are parts of the same system. Change one and you affect the other.	The physical dimension is very important. Moving around can help unblock a problem. Try going for a walk.
The person with the greatest flexibility of thinking and behaviour is likely to have the greatest influence.	If you're trying to resolve a dispute, you're probably going to need to be the most flexible of all the people involved
It is possible to find a positive intention behind all behaviour.	Protagonists may behave in what seem extreme ways, but they are seeking an outcome they desire. What is it? What would need to be true for them to behave the way they are behaving? How can their need be met a different way?
People have all the resources they need to make whatever changes they choose.	The parties can choose to resolve the dispute. The issue is whether they can accept the cost.
There is no such thing as failure, only feedback.	If you haven't found a solution yet, that's just feedback. Try something else.
There is a solution to every problem.	The dispute can be solved if everyone has the flexibility.
If it's possible in the world, then it's possible for me, if only I discover the "how."	Massive and complex disputes get solved. Yours can too. How were the others settled?
The identity of a person is different from the behaviour they demonstrate.	There's more to the participants than their behaviour in the dispute.

Energy flows where attention goes.	How can we shift the focus of attention away from the "difficult" areas and onto something conducive to collaborative behaviour?
People make the best decisions available to them at the time.	Parties in dispute, including us, make what seem to be bad choices, but they are doing the best they can. How can we help them make better decisions?

Steps to take

 Avoid forcing people to take sides. Allow the "third side" to play its role.

There are three sides to every argument: your side, my side and the right side.
Napoleon Hill

Dealing with "difficult" people

NLP urges us to believe there is no such thing as difficult people; we're just inflexible in dealing with them. Our experience of others is borne of our own inability to alter our behaviour in a radical enough way. That's a helpful, but stiff challenge. If the clock was turned back to 1938 and you were in Neville Chamberlain's shoes dealing with Adolf Hitler, what would you have done, if you had the skills in this book? That is a challenging question indeed. NLP thinking would say: Do what it takes to build rapport and then seek to influence the man toward a tolerable alternative, while developing flexibility through preparing alternative courses of action. Arguably, that's approximately what Chamberlain did and the Munich agreement was the best decision available to him at the time. We cannot deny that it would be hard, just as it may be hard for us in less extreme cases, to deal with some of the people we come across in our lives, especially when we are constrained by the situations in which we find ourselves, such as when we are part of an organisational relationship with another party.

Individuals only appear "difficult" to those who are deeply mismatched. To others more aligned with them, they could be the best of friends. If you are faced with dealing with somebody who you find difficult, where is the inflexibility in you that is stopping you from choosing to overcome the mismatch? Reviewing the presuppositions again:

The map is not the territory	If we experience the person as difficult, their map may be significantly different from ours.
The meaning of any communication is indicated by the response it gets.	If there are outbursts, our communication must carry significant meaning in the other person's model.
Mind and body are parts of the same system. Change one and you affect the other.	How can you disrupt the person's patterns by getting them to move around, for example? What if you have the difficult conversations while walking somewhere?
The person with the greatest flexibility of thinking and behaviour is likely to have the greatest influence.	In some respects, the difficult person has the greatest flexibility because their behaviour is so far from the norm. How can we approach them with just as radical an approach on our part?
It is possible to find a positive intention behind all behaviour.	What would need to be true for the difficult person to be acting the way they are acting?
People have all the resources they need to make whatever changes they choose.	We could choose to adapt to the difficult person. We may not want to, though, in which case we must take responsibility for the consequences of our choice.
There is no such thing as failure, only feedback.	If we haven't found a successful way to deal with the person yet, that's just feedback. Try something else.
There is a solution to every problem.	There is a way to deal with this person. We may decide it's not worth the cost to us, though.
If it's possible in the world, then it's possible for me, if only I discover the "how."	Who does cope with this individual? How do they manage?
The identity of a person is different from the behaviour they demonstrate.	What's behind the behaviour we perceive as difficult?
Energy flows where attention goes.	How can we shift the focus of attention away from the difficult areas and onto something conducive to collaborative behaviour?
People make the best decisions available to them at the time.	Despite how it might seem, the person is making the best decision they can.

Hard though it may be, attending to the difficult person is going to help (1), as will building rapport (6) and understanding their Values (7). Meanwhile, be clear about what's important to you (10). Use the shifting chairs process (9) to figure out what you could do differently (remember, you can only change yourself). Self-control (3) is likely to help you in dealing with difficult people, particularly in a work context, where rash actions may lead to legal problems.

In the end, you may decide to say, "No." Understand clearly what it is you want and the higher purpose that lies behind that. That will give you the strength and the grounds for saying "no" and often the beginnings of a negotiated compromise.

Keep in mind the cost of accommodating the difficult person, whatever the context. There may come a point where it's just not worth the effort. Attending to yourself means stopping the drain on your time and energy. Do whatever you have to do to finish it or get out of the situation. Life's too short to tolerate the problem for too long.

Before we finish on this topic: To whom are you a difficult person?

Commerce

Selling

The key to selling is finding out what matters to the person we want to sell to (7). What are their values? Once we have that information, we can shape our offer to suit. We want to find out the potential customer's values before we have said much about our offer. The skills of Attention to others (1) will help us do that. Rather than trying to sell your product, focus on solving the customer's problem.

To build rapport and tune in, we can draw on Wavelength (4), Filters (5), and Connection (6). Some work on our Self-awareness (9) will help us to assess how we come across and make changes if we feel they are necessary.

Steps to take

𝄃 Presuppose that there is a solution to the customer's need, and it is you and your offer.

Managing relationships where money is involved

What happens to our relationships when money is changing hands? The payment of cash or the creation of a contract to pay at some future time changes the nature of a relationship. The exchange of money creates expectations and shifts the point of balance between the people involved. The one providing the money, or representing the provider of money, is entitled to expect certain agreed things in return. For the sake of the relationship, it'll be best if they are indeed agreed. It is better to know where we stand. The most useful perspective is to be clear about the effect of money on the way the individuals concerned understand the relationship and what is important to them (7). Money changes the balance of values. Because of its exchange, one or other party assumes the right to place greater importance on some of their values than they do on those of the other participant.

At the outset, the parties will have different maps of how they expect the relationship to work, and some negotiation will be required. Being as clear as possible about the contractual terms will help ensure that the parties do have a shared model of how the relationship is expected to work.

In the case of a retail store, a combination of consumer laws and the brand values we associate with particular businesses ensure that the staff and the customer do have closely aligned models of how they expect business to be conducted. There is trust, and this is an important part of making trade possible.

Understanding the perspectives of the people involved (9) is important, as is being clear about what we want (10).

Steps to take

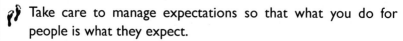 Take care to manage expectations so that what you do for people is what they expect.

Think through what's different in a relationship where money is changing hands. (Much of what we have covered is unaffected.) The main area where money has an impact is in the balance of attention to needs and values between the parties.

Family

Succeeding with partners

We have covered some points as we have gone along. Really, everything applies, including Love (12) and all of the NLP presuppositions:

The map is not the territory	Respect your partner's model of the world. However well matched you seem, you will have differences, some of them unconscious, and they may surface when you least expect them.
The meaning of any communication is indicated by the response it gets.	The effect of your communication or non-communication is your responsibility.
Mind and body are parts of the same system. Change one and you affect the other.	Remember the importance of non-verbal communication.
The person with the greatest flexibility of thinking and behaviour is likely to have the greatest influence.	And have the most successful partnership.
It is possible to find a positive intention behind all behaviour.	When your partner does something you don't like, find out what the underlying intention is and see if you can meet it another way.
People have all the resources they need to make whatever changes they choose.	That includes you. If you could change and don't, that's a choice.
There is no such thing as failure, only feedback.	If you haven't resolved an issue, you just haven't discovered the right way yet. Whatever happened is just feedback. It only becomes failure if you abandon this principle and give up.
There is a solution to every problem.	Relationships can be fixed if both parties want them to be fixed.
If it's possible in the world, then it's possible for me, if only I discover the "how."	Relationships with life partners have been known to work! It is possible. Even those for whom it seems easy may struggle more than they say.

The identity of a person is different from the behaviour they demonstrate.	Our behaviour in the moment may not reflect how we really are the majority of the time.
Energy flows where attention goes.	Focus on what you want in your relationship, not on what you don't want.
People make the best decisions available to them at the time.	There's no point in criticising a decision. It's better to explain how it doesn't work for you or what might be considered next time.

Balancing attention between yourself (10) and your partner (1) is clearly very important, as is your own clarity about what you want in life (11). Self-control (3) might be needed! An ability to think in a clear way about your and your partner's Values (7) and needs is going to help you make your relationship as good as you can make it. Working with your own and your partner's language patterns (8) will improve the effectiveness of the communication you have. Self-awareness (9) will also help.

Steps to take

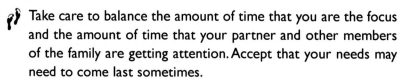 Take care to balance the amount of time that you are the focus and the amount of time that your partner and other members of the family are getting attention. Accept that your needs may need to come last sometimes.

Develop a shared view of your individual values, and understand where they match and where they don't. Sort out how you are going to run your lives so that all these values are met as much as possible. Think of ways of reshaping the things you do so that you meet more than one value with a single activity.

Parenting

Raising a family is probably the most difficult job in the world. Virginia Satir

Parenting is another massive subject and the applications of the material we have covered would fill a book in their own right. Everything will apply at one time or another. For example:

The map is not the territory	Respect children's models of the world from the very beginning.
The person with the greatest flexibility of thinking and behaviour is likely to have the greatest influence.	And be the most effective parent.
It is possible to find a positive intention behind all behaviour.	Even when the behaviour is very inconvenient for you. Be careful to distinguish between behaviour that you really want to displace and behaviour that just doesn't suit you at the time.
There is no such thing as failure, only feedback.	If you haven't achieved the result you wanted, try again.
If it's possible in the world, then it's possible for me, if only I discover the "how."	Take great care not to install limiting beliefs in children, and watch out for this happening at school.
Energy flows where attention goes.	Focus on what you want.
People make the best decisions available to them at the time.	Better to learn for the future than dwell on past mistakes.

As you begin to see the patterns in your family system more clearly, understand the problems better, and begin to act differently, it will help you to remember that whatever may have happened in the past, it was the best you and everyone else knew how to do at the time. Neither feeling guilty nor blaming others about past mistakes contributes anything to success in the present.

Be careful not to be so consumed by telling children what to do that you never enjoy them as people or give them the opportunity to enjoy you. Virginia Satir wrote: "I have met so many adults who have never known what it feels like to be enjoyed by another person. So instead of enjoying people themselves, they try to please, to get approval, and to keep from getting disapproval."

Paying attention to children (1) and respecting them is a good place to start in making a family work. Demonstrating self-control (3) and being balanced in our approach (11) helps. Just as with adults, children's language (8) often includes patterns that present opportunities to help them with their issues. Think about their values (7) and the values you are installing in them. Love (12), of course, is central.

Perhaps the most important relevance of the Steps to parenting is that, by adopting the skills in this book, you will be modelling for your children an effective way to live and relate to other people.

While writing this chapter, I have reflected on how challenging it is to make a marriage work and to raise a family. The Steps are by no means the whole answer, but I have found them to make a great deal of difference. Being able to understand what is going on at a deeper level has been tremendously helpful—a life-saver, in a sense.

> **Steps to take**
> Find ways to make sure your family members take time to enjoy each other as individuals.

My dream is to make families a place where adults with high self-esteem can develop. Virginia Satir

When you apply the Steps

When you apply the Steps to the areas we have covered, you will be successful. You will also gain in your experience of the skills and be effective in your use of them in other situations. The great thing about this skill set, in contrast with many other areas of expertise, is that once you have learned the Steps in one context, that experience maps across to other applications.

We have covered a great deal in this book. In any situation, you are only going to have so much time to use what you have learned. Choose the most appropriate element for the particular situation. Often, you will need only one aspect of one topic to make the critical difference. Rather than pretend we have infinite capacity, I prefer to recognise the constraints of time that apply to us. We need to focus. Take care to choose the most effective approach at any given time. With practice, you will use more of the skills unconsciously in ways that will help you.

> **Steps to take**
> Reflect on how the Steps apply to other applications in your life—ones we haven't covered.

Applying the Steps

A reminder of the Steps

1: Attention to others: shifting our focus

2: Attitude: using the presuppositions of NLP

3: Self-control: with peripheral vision and meditation

4: Wavelength: VAK or A-D

5: Filters: noticing their effects

6: Connection: managing rapport

7: Values: using the levels model and Maslow's Hierarchy of Needs

8: Language: unpacking deletions, distortions, and generalisations

9: Self-awareness: working with perceptions

10: Attention to ourselves: choosing what we want, being peaceful

11: Balance: resolving conflict inside and outside

12: Love: adding the final ingredient

Relating to you

What situation of yours will you transform first?

What will you do differently after reading this chapter?

Epilogue: Now at your side

And to make an end is to make a beginning. T.S. Eliot

So there we have it: A systematic approach to success in personal and professional relationships. With it, you will be able to unlock many problems and opportunities. Like Joseph Jaworski, you may well see "relationship as the organising principle of the universe," and so recognise the importance of what we have shared together—a treasure trove to transform your world by enriching your relationships with other people, while approaching a deeper understanding of life itself.

No doubt I could have included more, and I personally hope and expect to go on learning, but as a former colleague once said: "The excellent is the enemy of the good enough." Good now is infinitely more useful than perfection that takes forever to arrive.

Much of the material has been drawn from NLP, and I have touched on its application to coaching, its usual focus. I would encourage you to explore that subject further by reading some of the many books available or, even better, by attending some courses. I have suggested some books in the Bibliography. Take care choosing the training provider you select: Look for values that align with your own and decide whether you are more interested in techniques, or developing as an individual—your personal "journey." In my view, that's the main distinction between one provider and another. Both approaches have their place, but for me, personal growth is the most important aspect. If you're doubtful about whether learning about coaching would be useful to you, think about this: As sportspeople become better at their game, do they get more coaching or less?

Maybe you haven't done much with the material in this book at the practical level yet. If you have, great; if not, well, now is the time to start. Reading and understanding will not be enough on their own for you to gain the benefits you could gain. If I've done even a half-decent job of writing, you will have realised how effective the skills are. I hope you gain as much from learning them as I have, and I hope I have sparked your interest and that you will explore further. As Richard Bandler said: "The things I'm teaching you work, but I want you to think about what else might work even better. There is a huge difference between learning some things and discovering what there is still to learn. That is the difference that makes the difference."

The 12 Steps, when practised in full or even only in part, add up to tremendous power. You probably don't realise yet just what a sharp instrument you have in your hands. As you learn the skills and apply them to your life and your relationships, you will see just how powerful they are and what an edge you have.

With power comes responsibility. Your intention matters. Were it to be to win at someone else's expense, then you might succeed in the short term, but your lack of integrity would defeat you in the long run. The power of these skills would make your undoing happen more quickly. On the other hand, if your intention is to achieve a win for the other person, a win for yourself, and if possible, a win for the world at large, you will succeed, probably way beyond what you imagine. Use your new powers with integrity and love. They will only work for you in the long run if you do.

Let me refer back to the classic where we started:

The principles taught in this book will work only when they come from the heart. I am not advocating a bag of tricks. I am talking about a new way of life.
Dale Carnegie

In beginning this book, I knew there were only two things in doubt: Whether I would be able to present the skills in a manner that would make it possible for you to learn them; and whether you would be ready to take them on. The skills work. If they didn't, they wouldn't be so widely used. They provide a powerful resource, dependable foundation, and system of life-long learning and so truly deliver balance, peace, and "relationship mastery." I hope I have done a reasonable job of the first challenge of conveying the material. You can be the judge of that. The second task is completely in your hands. You have read this far, so I have grounds for optimism.

Thank you for reading my book. If I can help you further in applying your learning to your particular circumstances, please get in touch at david@davidfraser.com or visit www.davidfraser.com.

A suggestion

If your life has been touched by what I have written, or you feel this book can help solve the problems of the world, or both, then I invite you to bring this book respectfully to the attention of people you know who may benefit.

Acknowledgements

The sources and influences I have drawn on in creating this book are so varied that recording them all is beyond me. If I have included your idea or borrowed your turn of phrase without appropriate recognition, then please contact me for proper acknowledgement in the future.

The story of the book as much as I can relate it begins with the psychologist Carl Gustav Jung (1875–1961). His thinking is the foundation of much of the material. Next are Abraham Maslow (1908–70), founder of Humanistic Psychology, Virginia Satir (1916–88), who worked with troubled families to great effect, and Milton Erickson (1901–80), a groundbreaking therapist and a supreme example of ability to relate to other people. In the 1970s, Richard Bandler and John Grinder created the field of Neuro-Linguistic Programming (NLP), which in turn forms the backbone of the approach in this book. Robert Dilts built on that work and, among other things, developed some of the frameworks we use. More general references include M. Scott Peck (*The Road Less Traveled*), Stephen R. Covey (*The 7 Habits of Highly Effective People*), Eckhart Tolle (*The Power of Now*), Wayne Dyer (*Manifest Your Destiny*), and Dale Carnegie (*How to Win Friends and Influence People*).

The influence of teachers from whom I have learned directly is everywhere in these pages. I would like to thank Stuart Hepburn of ThinkGlobal, David Shephard (co-author of *Presenting Magically*), Sue Knight (*NLP at Work*), and Toby and Kate McCartney of West One NLP, John Sturrock and Pamela Lyall of Core Solutions, Frank Farrelly (*Provocative Therapy*), Ken Cloke (*Mediating Dangerously* and *The Crossroads of Conflict*), and William Ury (*Getting to Yes* and *The Third Side*).

A number of other people have been influential, including Peter Thomson and the numerous authors of Nightingale Conant audio programmes from whom I have learned a great deal over the years. I would especially mention Earl Nightingale (*Lead the Field*), Thomas Leonard (*The 28 Principles of Attraction*), Ted Nicholas (*Magic Words that Grow Your Business*), and Richard Koch (*The 80:20 Principle*).

The rest of the ingredients come from a West-of-Scotland upbringing, a sprinkling of Buddhist teaching, a varied career, and 47 years' experience of life.

As this book began to come together, a number of people generously gave of their time to support the project. Despite having read countless acknowledgements in books over the years, I had no inkling that engaging one's friends and colleagues in helping develop a book could be such a humbling experience. The amount of care, attention, and love they have shown has taken me on an emotional journey and been an influence in itself. These people are Barbara Robertson, Olivia Giles, Eric Young, Madeleine Allen, Martin Jones, Calum Macaulay, Marnie Roadburg, Eleni Sarantinou, Mike Orr, Julian Thomas, Hillary Sillitto, Brian Martin, Miriam King, Karen Mason, Morag Cook, Florence Madden, Carol Moor, and Liz Walsh. More than anything, these people have shown that the subject matters. I also want to acknowledge the contributions and wholehearted engagement of numerous participants in workshops I have led, from whom I have learned a great deal.

I am grateful to Shelley Lieber, Mark Bloom, Janet Aiossa, and Liz Handy for their great assistance in the preparation of this edition, to Lynda Gillespie, Gillian Dick, and Teresa Morrow for their support, and to Charles Handy for his interest and wise counsel. Seth Godin's writing has also been a continuing source of insight. Very special thanks are due to Sir Kenneth Calman for contributing the Foreword.

Many other people have been an inspiration. Some I am unlikely ever to meet. Others are more personal and my late mother and father come to mind.

My wife Catriona has been the biggest supporter of this book. Without her tolerance and sacrifice, it would not have come to fruition, and much more would have gone wrong besides. Catriona has contributed willingly and with insight throughout and devoted many hours to discussion and review.

Finally, I turn to my three children, who have had to compete with this book for my attention. They are the greatest inspiration of all. One of them (age six at the time) even suggested a title *Start To Get On*, which showed a remarkable grasp of the subject for one so young.

Bibliography

Suggested introductory, general reading is indicated by a *

Bandler, Richard, Andreas, Connirae, and Andreas, Steve (Eds.)
Using Your Brain for a Change, Real People Press, Boulder, Colorado, 1985
One of a number of accessible books from one of the founders of NLP.

Bandler, Richard and Grinder, John *Patterns of the Hypnotic Techniques of Milton H. Erickson, M.D., Volume I*, Grinder & Associates, Scotts Valley, 1975
Modelling of Erickson's techniques. Of wider interest for the workings of the mind, particularly in relation to the roles of representation systems. A technical book.

Bandler, Richard and Grinder, John *The Structure of Magic, Volume I*, Science and Behaviour Books, Palo Alto, 1975
The first NLP book. Documents the Meta-model. Rigorous and detailed, so prepare for a technical read. More recent books by Richard Bandler and others are an easier place to start.

Bandler, Richard and Grinder, John *The Structure of Magic, Volume II*, Science and Behaviour Books, Palo Alto, 1976
Implications and use of the different representational systems in the mind. Includes application to family therapy. Same style as Volume I. A technical and rigorous read.

Benson, Nigel C. *Introducing Psychology*, Icon Books, Royston, 2004
An accessible overview of the main strands of psychology. Includes Maslow's work.

* Carnegie, Dale *How to Win Friends and Influence People* (Revised Edition), Vermilion, London, 2006
The classic on relationships. Probably the most widely read book on this list. Just as vital as when first published in 1937.

Charvet, Shelle Rose *Words that Change Minds (2nd Edition)*, Kendall/Hunt, Dubuque, 1997
Devoted to filtering patterns (Metaprogrammes).

Cloke, Ken *The Crossroads of Conflict: A journey into the Heart of Dispute Resolution*, Janis Publications, Calgary, 2006
Presents a "unified theory for resolving conflict," rooted in a deep understanding.

Collins, Jim *Good to Great*, Random House, London, 2001
A study of what made the difference in what became great businesses.

Cooper, Lynne *Business NLP for Dummies*, John Wiley & Sons, Chichester, 2008
An introduction to NLP, focused on the business reader, in the usual For Dummies *style.*

Covey, Stephen R. *The 7 Habits of Highly Effective People*, Simon & Schuster, London, 1989
A modern classic on making the most of one's life. A portion of this book is about relationships.

Dilts, Robert *Changing Belief Systems with NLP*, Meta Publications, Capitola, 1990
Detailed and convincing in typical Robert Dilts style.

Dilts, Robert *Sleight of Mouth: The Magic of Conversational Belief Change*, Meta Publications, Capitola, 1999
An accessible book on language and beliefs.

Dyer, Wayne *Manifest Your Destiny*, Element, London, 1997
One of many from the same author making sense of spirituality and other matters.

Farrelly, Frank and Brandsma, Jeff *Provocative Therapy*, Meta Publications, Capitola, 1974
A book for therapists and those who want to stop pussy-footing around, with much to learn from Frank about effective and loving use of directness and humour.

Fisher, Roger, Ury, William, and Patton, Bruce *Getting to Yes*, Random House, London, 1991
The standard on negotiation.

Ford, Debbie *The Dark Side of the Light Chasers*, Hodder and Stoughton, London, 2001
Takes us toward wholeness by integrating those parts of ourselves we sometimes deny. A profound, influential, and challenging book.

Gladwell, Malcolm *The Tipping Point: How Little Things Can Make a Big Difference*, Abacus, London, 2001
How conditions can suddenly become right for significant change.

Goleman, Daniel *Emotional Intelligence*, Bloomsbury, London, 1996
Gave rise to the topic of "emotional intelligence."

Grinder, John, Delozier, Judith, and Bandler, Richard *Patterns of the Hypnotic Techniques of Milton H. Erickson, M.D., Volume II*, Grinder & Associates, Scotts Valley, 1977
Further modelling of Erickson's techniques. Again of wider interest for the workings of the mind, particularly in relation to the roles of representation systems. A technical book.

* Hyde, Maggie and McGuinness, Michael *Introducing Jung*, Icon Books, Royston, 2004
A quick and accessible way to an overview of Carl Jung's work and ideas.

James, Tad and Shephard, David *Presenting Magically: Transforming Your Stage Presence with NLP*, Crown House Publishing, Carmarthen, 2001
Focused on the use of NLP in public speaking of various kinds, but with a wider relevance and much useful detail on aspects of NLP, breathing techniques, and other practical help.

James, Tad and Woodsmall, Wyatt *Time Line Therapy and The Basis of Personality*, Meta Publications, Capitola, 1988
Covers time line work (a powerful coaching technique), metaprogrammes, and values. In-depth and readable treatment. Conveys the far-reaching implications of these topics.

Jaworksi, Joseph *Synchronicity: The Inner Path of Leadership*, Berrett-Koehler, San Francisco, 1996
Profound messages about organisational learning and an inspiring account of the author's personal journey.

Johnson, Kerry L. *Selling with NLP*, Nicholas Brealey Publishing, London, 1993
Covers the use of NLP in sales in a thorough and readable way.

Kahane, Adam *Power and Love: A Theory and Practice of Social Change*, Berrett-Koehler, San Francisco, 2010
Makes a compelling case for the importance of combining love and power, just as in using two legs to walk.

* Knight, Sue *NLP at Work (3rd Edition)*, Nicholas Brealey Publishing, London, 2009
A comprehensive introduction and reference. Authentically Sue. A good place to start.

Koch, Richard *The 80:20 Principle (audio programme)*, Nightingale Conant, Paignton, 2003
Sets out the benefits of focusing on the "vital few."

Leonard, Thomas *The 28 Principles of Attraction (audio programme)*, Nightingale Conant, Niles, 2002
Includes principles for relating to people. Very pragmatic and down-to-earth.

Nairn, Rob *Diamond Mind: Psychology of Meditation (2nd Edition)*, Kairon Press, Kalk Bay, 2007
A short book on meditation. A handy introduction.

Nicholas, Ted *Magic Words That Grow Your Business (audio programme)*, Nightingale Conant, Niles, 1997
An authority on the use of language to put a message across and on how to relate to people.

Nightingale, Earl *Lead the Field (audio programme)*, Nightingale Conant, Niles, 1996
Classic of the audio programme industry, covering principles of success and "the strangest secret"—i.e., "We become what we think about."

O'Connor, Joseph and Lages, Andrea *Coaching with NLP*, Element, London, 2004
An accessible, general-purpose book on coaching using NLP techniques and ideas.

Palmer, Parker J. *The Courage to Teach*, Jossey-Bass, San Francisco, 2007
Makes the case for reconnecting who we are with what we do. Written in the context of teaching, but of much wider relevance.

Peck, M. Scott *The Road Less Travelled*, Arrow, London, 1983
Popular modern classic on love and spirituality from a psychology perspective. A full and profound read.

Prior, Robin and O'Connor, Joseph *NLP and Relationships*, Element, London, 2002
Focused on relationships with spouses, significant others, life partners, etc.

* Ready, Romilla and Burton, Kate *NLP for Dummies*, John Wiley & Sons, Chichester, 2004
An accessible and detailed introduction to NLP.

Rosen, Sydney (Ed) *My Voice Will Go with You: The Teaching Tales of Milton H. Erickson, M.D.*, Norton, New York, 1982
Amounts to a loving perspective on Milton Erickson's life, work, and beliefs. Has something for everyone.

Satir, Virginia *Peoplemaking*, Souvenir Press, London, 1978
A classic on the challenges of family life—down-to-earth and uplifting in equal measure. Just as valid now as when written in 1972.

Senge, Peter *The Fifth Discipline (Revised Edition)*, Random House, London, 2006
Influential and rounded treatment of the characteristics of learning organisations and the art of change, including the concept of "personal mastery" as a vital ingredient.

Tolle, Eckhart *The Power of Now*, Hodder and Stoughton, London, 2005
About mindfulness and living in the present. Life-changing, potentially, if you can stand apart long enough from the "voice in your head" to realise it's not you. Otherwise, come back later.

Ury, William *The Third Side*, Penguin, London, 2000
On the importance of third parties in managing conflict and resolving disputes.

Ury, William *The Power of a Positive No*, Hodder and Stoughton, London, 2007
A book devoted to making a success when your answer is "no."

Glossary

Anchoring Associating a state with a stimulus.

Associated The state of being engaged in a situation, experiencing it directly through our senses.

Auditory Representational system associated with the sense of hearing.

Auditory-Digital (A-D) Representational system associated with internal dialogue (self-talk).

Beliefs Elements of our model of the world treated as facts and the reference for the actions we take.

Break state Use of a movement or distraction to change emotional state.

Coaching Helping clients to be successful, and helping them determine what success means for them.

Congruence Having all parts working in harmony without conflict.

Dissociated The state of being disengaged from a situation, observing as if an outsider, and disconnected from emotion.

Ecology The consequence of our thoughts and actions in the system of which we are a part. NLP shorthand for our effect on others.

Eye accessing cues Movements of our eyes that suggest visual, auditory, kinaesthetic, or auditory-digital (self-talk) thinking.

Filter A (largely unconscious) thinking process that determines what we pay attention to and how we respond to our environment.

Foveal vision Visual awareness focused on what's directly in front of us—associated with stress response (see also Peripheral vision).

Incongruence Internal conflict, resulting in inconsistent behaviour.

Kinaesthetic Representational system associated with the sense of touch and feelings.

Linguistic Pertaining to language.

Mediation Process of facilitated negotiation conducted by a neutral, non-judgmental third party.

Meta-model A system for working with the deletions, generalisations, and distortions in spoken and written language, reflecting unresourceful aspects of our model of the world.

Metaprogramme NLP term for filter.

Modelling The process of analysing the means of achieving useful results so that those results can be replicated. Also, demonstrating a way of doing something to someone—usually with the intention of unconsciously guiding them—leading by example.

Neuro Pertaining to mental and sensory activity.

Neuro-Linguistic Programming Literally, the patterning of behaviour through sensory experience, mental activity, and language. The study of the structure of subjective experience, the nature of excellence, and the difference that makes the difference—a means of continual learning. Often also taken to mean some of the techniques that flow from that study.

Pacing Allowing another person to lead in a relationship by respecting and following the values they apply and the style of communication they use.

Perceptual positions A process of moving between the various positions in a situation: our own (first position); that of the other person (second position); that of an interested but unspecified observer (third position); and if appropriate, that of specific onlookers (fourth position). The perspectives are explored in each case, with the intention of generating new possibilities for the person in first position.

Peripheral vision Visual awareness expanded to the fullest possible extent—associated with relaxation response (see also Foveal vision).

Preferred representational system A thinking style favoured by an individual.

Presupposition Something assumed in advance. The "Presuppositions of NLP" are a set of empowering beliefs found to lead to useful results.

Programming The process of setting up mostly unconscious and often repetitive patterns of behaviour, whether useful or problematic.

Rapport A state shared by two or more people in which there is a feeling of respect, trust, and emotional connection.

Representational systems Channels of thinking applied to information received from specific senses or internal dialogue.

Resources Anything that can help to achieve an outcome, including past experiences that may usefully be reinterpreted.

Sensory acuity NLP term for the ability to pick up what's going on in our environment, through unconscious non-verbal signals, for example.

State The condition of a person at a given time, both physical and emotional.

Strategy A sequence of thinking and behaviour steps to achieve a result.

Therapy A process in which a client seeks relief from psychological or physical pain.

Third-sider One who takes the role of intermediary in a dispute and acts to resolve the issue, or one who supports the parties as they do so themselves.

VAK Common abbreviation for visual, auditory and kinaesthetic representational systems as a set.

Value Something that is important to us, whether known consciously or unconsciously.

Visual Representational system associated with the sense of sight.

The Author

Dr David Fraser is a leading authority on relationship skills in professional and personal life. With his breadth of knowledge, an engineer's talent for organising systematic and reliable solutions, and an ability to write in an interesting, direct, and readable way, David is well positioned to address the age-old challenge of how to build effective relationships with other people.

David has a track record of pioneering new approaches to old problems. He has delivered major projects for government and private sector clients in challenging situations and set up a number of entrepreneurial ventures. He is a business owner, and a Chartered Engineer with a First Class Honours degree and a PhD from Glasgow University and an MBA from Strathclyde University. He is a qualified commercial mediator and a Neuro-Linguistic Programming (NLP) Master Practitioner and has trained with leading proponents of these disciplines.

David applies his unusual blend of expertise to supporting disparate groups working together in complex circumstances, including major collaborative projects and matters of national importance. In addition to his work on relationship management with corporate clients, David runs workshop and coaching programmes on relationship skills and leadership for both organisations and individuals, focusing on the potential to leverage results. David also finds the approach set out in *Relationship Mastery: A Business Professional's Guide* to be extremely helpful in the home and family environment.

David lives with his wife and three children in Glasgow, Scotland and sails on the West Coast of Scotland when time permits.

For more information, see www.drdavidfraser.com or email david@davidfraser.com.

Never doubt that a small group of thoughtful, committed citizens can change the world. Indeed, it is the only thing that ever has.

–Margaret Mead

Lightning Source UK Ltd.
Milton Keynes UK
UKOW05f1540110515

251254UK00002B/15/P